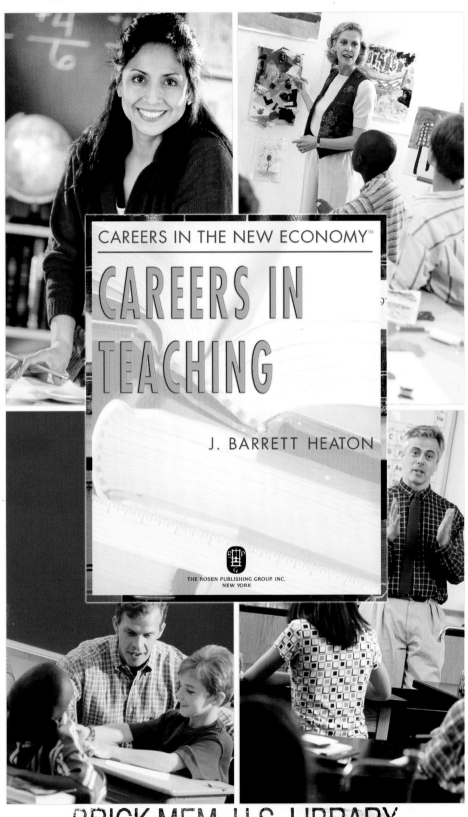

CAREERS IN THE NEW ECONOMY™

CAREERS IN TEACHING

J. BARRETT HEATON

THE ROSEN PUBLISHING GROUP, INC.
NEW YORK

To all those who helped me as I put this book together—especially my wife, Megumi, and my daughter, Phoebe

Published in 2005 by The Rosen Publishing Group, Inc.
29 East 21st Street, New York, NY 10010

Library of Congress Cataloging-in-Publication Data
Heaton, J. Barrett.
Careers in teaching/J. Barrett Heaton.
    p. cm.—(Careers in the new economy)
Includes bibliographical references and index.
ISBN 1-4042-0250-1 (library binding)
1. Teaching—Vocational guidance—United States.
I. Title. II. Series.
LB1775.2.H43 2005

                                                2004011249

Manufactured in the United States of America

Photo Credits: Cover, pp. 1, 3, 4, 16, 33, 48, 55, 62, 69, 75, 92, 102, 117, 126, 128, 140, 141, 142 © Comstock, Inc.; pp. 6, 12, 38, 57, 93 © National Center for Education Statistics, U.S. Department of Education; p. 30 © California Department of Education; p. 86 © Hunter College of the City University of New York; p. 119 courtesy of American Association for Employment in Education, Inc

Additional Credits: pp. 8–9, Ben Franklin Lesson Plan courtesy of Discovery Education, a division of Discovery Communications, Inc.; p. 111, table of estimated average annual salary of teachers in public elementary and secondary schools, by state, 1969–1970 to 2001–2002, courtesy of National Center for Education Statistics, U.S. Department of Education.

Designer: Nelson Sá; **Editor:** Charles Hofer; **Photo Researcher:** Nelson Sá

CONTENTS

CHAPTER 1

CONSIDERING A CAREER IN TEACHING

Teaching is an occupation for millions of individuals around the world. Because the people who teach are so diverse, it is difficult to generalize about who they are, what kind of characteristics they share, and why they became involved with the field of education. However, as you consider a career in education, you will gradually define just what teaching means to you. This book aims to help you clarify your understanding of the field of education as well as your potential relationship to it. Particularly due to the great demand for teachers of all levels and in all regions, you should realize that teaching offers an opportunity for you to achieve a great deal of personal satisfaction while securing financial stability.

HOW WIDESPREAD IS THE TEACHING PROFESSION?

There are more teachers in the world than any other single profession. In the United States, every young person is entitled by law to what is called a free appropriate public education. Legislation passed by the federal government has mandated that this education continue through the high school level for all individuals, regardless of race, culture, disability, and religion. In fact, the youth of America are required by law to stay in school until they are sixteen years old. Laws such as these ensure that thousands of teachers will remain in demand for decades to come.

STATISTICS AT A GLANCE

The total population of the United States has increased dramatically since the 1980s. The 2000 U.S. census recorded some 280 million people living in the United States. That same census estimates that the population will swell to 300 million by the year 2010. The number of students has grown right along with this general population increase. As evidence of this, the National Center for Education Statistics (NCES) reports that in 2001, approximately 54 million K–12 (kindergarten through twelfth grade) students attended public and private schools. Although some 45.4 million students of the same ages attended school in 1988, the NCES predicts the number will reach 56.4 million by 2013. All of these figures suggest that the number of teachers needed to educate this growing population must increase as well.

THE ROLE OF EDUCATION

Even if education weren't such a huge field in terms of the sheer number of people involved, it would still play a central role in the health and character of the United States. Governments, companies, communities, and families all struggle to understand the dramatic changes that continue to affect their lives. These changes include developments in

site index | ED.gov **NCES** National Center for Education Statistics [Search NCE] Go

the
condition
of **education**

This website is an integrated collection of the indicators and analyses published in *The Condition of Education* 2000, 2001, 2002, 2003 and 2004. Some indicators may have been updated since they originally appeared in print. You can also download/view a PDF of the entire Condition of Education 2004 report.

HIGHLIGHTS From COE 2004	**COMMISSIONER'S STATEMENT** Summary of findings
INDICATOR LIST Access indicators and supporting material	**BRIEFING SLIDES** Of NCES commissioner (PDF, 667 kb)
SITE MAP A visual overview	**PRESS GUIDE** Information for reporters
PRINT EDITIONS List of COE publications in PDF format	**USER'S GUIDE** How to use this site

Quick Jump to: GO

NCES
Headlines
- UPDATED! Education Finance Statistics School District Peer Tool
- JUST RELEASED! Education Statistics Quarterly-Vol. 5 Issue 4
- NEW REPORT: Teacher Attrition and Mobility

NCES Home | Publications | Surveys & Programs | Quick Tables & Figures | Data Tools
Search | Help | News Flash | NCES Staff | Contact NCES | Site Index

National Center for Education Statistics
Institute of Education Sciences, U.S. Dept. of Education
map) 1990 K Street, NW, Washington, DC 20006, USA, Phone: (202) 502-7300

The Internet is an invaluable resource where you can learn more about the world of teaching. Web sites, such as this one from the National Center for Education Statistics (NCES), offer a wealth of information on the current state of education in the United States.

technology, the meeting and mixing of world cultures, the nature of the world after the end of the Cold War, and the rise of terrorism. The ideas, values, and information regarding these and other changes must be introduced through education in order for them to be better understood by society at large. The classroom provides a forum where diverse opinions and perspectives can be expressed, where research can be conducted, and where the search for truth can be engaged, without motivation from a political standpoint or from a thirst for capitalist profit.

Education is, in fact, the means by which any nation prepares for its future. An investment in its youth through education will affect the productivity of the country's workers, the intelligence of its thinkers, the justice of its judicial system, the viability of its technology with regard to the environment, and its peace with other nations.

Teaching is the central career in the field of education. Although a variety of jobs need to be performed in support of public and private schools, the teachers in the classroom are those in direct contact with members of future generations. Teachers can help shape these young leaders, writers, musicians, scientists, and parents. The roles educators play and the environments they create for learning and interaction can have significant and lasting effects on their students.

JUST WHAT DO TEACHERS DO?

Although you have spent countless hours with teachers over the course of your life, what you see and hear in the classroom is really just one aspect of the whole experience of being a teacher. Of course, teachers have a lot to do outside of the classroom as well, including preparing for classes, educating themselves, dealing

Sample Lesson Plan

Creating a lesson plan is just one example of how you can create a fun yet productive classroom environment. The following is an example of a daily lesson plan that could be created by a teacher.

TITLE OF LESSON PLAN
Ben Franklin

DURATION
One class period

GRADE LEVEL
6-8

SUBJECT
U.S. History

OBJECTIVES
Students will understand the following:
1. Ben Franklin is known, among other things, for his wit and wisdom.
2. Franklin published an almanac annually for 25 years.
3. He scattered proverbs (or aphorisms), short sayings that spoke the truth, throughout the almanac.

MATERIALS
For this lesson, you will need:
1. Provide a brief biographical sketch of Ben Franklin:
   - Born in Boston in 1706
   - Self-educated
   - As a teenager, studied printing in his brother's newspaper shop
   - Independent; he went off on his own to Philadelphia
   - Became a printer and a civic leader
   - After retirement (at 42), invented the lightning rod, bifocal lenses; discovered electricity
   - Worked extensively in public affairs
   - Died in 1790

2. Explain that above and beyond all the achievements just listed, Franklin was also a writer. He was known, among other writings, for his annual almanac, into which he sprinkled proverbs, or aphorisms—some of which Franklin had heard and then modified, others of which he created.

3. Distribute to students a list of some or all of the following proverbs by Franklin from *Poor Richard's Almanack*:
   - To err is human, to repent divine; to persist devilish.
   - At the working man's house hunger looks in, but dares not enter.
   - There are no ugly loves, nor handsome prisons.
   - Love your Neighbor; yet don't pull down your Hedge.
   - No gains without pains.

DISCUSSION QUESTIONS

1. Explain how Benjamin Franklin was "the quintessential American" of his time. Who would you call the quintessential American of our time? Why?

2. How did Franklin shape the Enlightenment in America? Discuss his use of reason to explain things and conduct his life.

3. Was Franklin a traitor to England? Were his actions in support of the colonies justifiable? Debate your answers.

4. Defend or criticize Franklin's response to his son William's leadership in the Loyalist movement.

5. Compare and contrast Franklin's views and actions regarding slavery with those of other colonial leaders such as Washington and Jefferson.

6. Discuss what Franklin's epitaph should be.

EVALUATION

You can evaluate students' work using the following three-point rubric:
- Three points: full and clear paraphrase; original proverb, which matches sense of Franklin's, with striking imagery; no errors in grammar, usage, and mechanics
- Two points: adequate paraphrase; original proverb, which comes close to sense of Franklin's; some errors in grammar, usage, and mechanics
- One point: inadequate paraphrase; original proverb only partially related in meaning to Franklin's; many errors in grammar, usage, and mechanics.

with their students' parents, interacting with their fellow teachers, and meeting with school administrators (principal, department heads, etc.). A teacher's job can be broken down into three types of tasks: interpersonal, creative, and administrative.

INTERPERSONAL TASKS

As a student, it is easy to observe teachers interacting with people because that is what they do in the classroom. However, teachers have many other individuals with whom they need to communicate, including fellow teachers, school administration members such as principals, and especially students' parents. All of this interaction requires a broad set of skills, including listening, presenting information, clarifying goals, and advising. Teachers interact with such a variety of people that communication skills become all the more crucial. Additionally, teachers have to make themselves available for meetings and must foster positive relationships to make their interactions work. Communication is certainly a central aspect of teachers' jobs.

CREATIVE TASKS

A teacher's creativity becomes most apparent in his or her lessons. Lessons can take hours of planning, including the selection of material to cover, the preparation of lecture notes, and the creation of handouts.

However, lesson planning is only one aspect of the creativity teachers exercise. Teachers, especially those working with younger students, create a classroom environment using decorations, posters, light, plants, and other living displays such as aquariums. The use of such materials can help students relax and enjoy the process of learning. Teachers may even experiment with seating arrangements to encourage different types of discussions.

With the rise of affordable technology, teachers increasingly have access to multimedia materials such as computers, DVD players, video cameras, and stereo systems that may be used to present material. Increasingly, teachers can incorporate creative projects into their classes that encourage students to use such technology as a means of realizing their own ideas as well.

Creativity is obviously a key element of any teacher's work. As teachers gain experience, they come to understand the entire school year as a cycle, with a beginning, a middle, and an end. Lessons are actually just small parts of a broader picture that teachers create for their students. The entire sequence of lessons is known as a curriculum. For example, a single course like U.S. history may be thought of as a curriculum designed for eleventh graders; all of the courses an eleventh grader takes that year may be considered as a curriculum as well. Teachers must be creative as they design curricula in order to fit their lessons into this larger context. Good teachers let their students know about the larger picture and how everyday learning fits into it.

Teaching style is also something that educators must create and gradually develop each school year. Some teachers are strong and strict, while some are more soft-spoken. But all teachers express an individual personality. One's teaching style can have a lot to do with success in the classroom.

ADMINISTRATIVE TASKS

Teachers face a significant amount of paperwork. Much of it revolves around student grades. Educators have to grade papers, keep records of grades, calculate grades, and may even have to add comments to each student's report card. The grades that students receive reflect a combination of performance on homework assignments,

Student Name _____ Grade _____ Year _____

This report card provides summary information of your child's progress in school. It is very important that you also talk with the teacher for more detailed information about your child's progress. We know that by working together, we can do our best for your child.

		REPORT PERIOD			
		1	2	3	4
ATTENDANCE	Present				
	Absent				
	Tardy				
Your child's progress could be helped by	Attending School Regularly				
	Getting to School on Time				

ESOL: English for Speakers of Other Languages

EXCEPTIONAL STUDENT EDUCATION

Your child has an Individual Education Plan (IEP). Throughout the report card, an asterisk (*) denotes an IEP goal. The academic code indicates your child's progress toward meeting this goal.

EXPECTED BEHAVIORS   Areas below are marked 'N' if improvement is needed.

- Follows School and Classroom Rules
- Follows Directions
- Is Prepared for Class
- Listens Attentively
- Participates in Class Activities
- Works Without Disturbing Others
- Completes Work in Assigned Time
- Completes Homework Assignments
- Shows Effort to do Best Work
- Works Cooperatively with Others
- Takes Care of Personal and School Property
- Respects Others and is Courteous
- Practices Self Control
- Respects Authority
- Behaves Appropriately in Art
- Behaves Appropriately in Music
- Behaves Appropriately in Physical Education

PROGRESS CODES

K - 2 Codes	3 - 5 Codes
E = Excellent	A = Excellent
S = Satisfactory	B = Good
N = Needs Improvement/More Time	C = Satisfactory
U = Unsatisfactory (ALERT: Unsatisfactory Benchmark Progress)	N = Needs Improvement
	U = Unsatisfactory (ALERT: Unsatisfactory Benchmark Progress)

INSTRUCTIONAL LEVEL CODE	AL = Above Grade Level
	OL = On Grade Level
	BL = Below Grade Level (ALERT: Unsatisfactory Benchmark Progress)

Academic grades reflect progress on grade level expectations.

REPORT PERIOD		1	2	3	4
READING	Instructional Level				
	Academic Progress				
WRITTEN COMMUNICATION	Instructional Level				
	Academic Progress				
MATHEMATICS	Instructional Level				
	Academic Progress				
SCIENCE/HEALTH	Academic Progress				
SOCIAL STUDIES	Academic Progress				
ART	Academic Progress				
MUSIC	Academic Progress				
PHYSICAL EDUCATION	Academic Progress				
PARENT COMMUNICATIONS					
	Date(s) Conference Requested				
	Date(s) Conference Held				
	Date(s) Progress Alert Sent				
	Enclosure(s)				

Placement for the 20____ -20____ School Year: Grade _____

The role of assessment, such as report cards, has changed a great deal over the years and has become much more complicated. Whereas years ago, teachers might simply report on their students' grades, today many teachers have to report on students' behavior and progress.

tests, quizzes, in-class participation, and/or effort. Some of these scores are easy to determine, while others are more difficult because they involve impressions and opinions of students.

Outside of grades, a number of other administrative tasks must be performed by teachers. Such tasks can include attendance records, reports on student behavior, evaluations of other teachers' work, and self-evaluations. Increasingly, teachers are using computers when completing these administrative tasks.

CHARACTERISTICS OF A GOOD TEACHER

Everyone has his or her own answer to the following question: What qualities should teachers possess to be effective? There are many opinions on the subject, but it remains clear that teachers are role models. Putting their personal lives aside, teachers must project a certain level of decency and respect for students. Almost invariably, teachers must be tolerant of a wide range of student behavior. They also need to remain patient in the face of difficulty. In addition to these qualities, create your own list of the characteristics that you feel teachers should have. If you are in a more critical mood, you might even put together a quick list of the personality traits that teachers shouldn't have or that impair their ability to succeed with their students. As you consider becoming a teacher, you should realize that even if you don't believe you possess all of the qualities of a good teacher right now, you can develop and acquire these qualities through hard work and commitment.

THE STUDENT TEACHER

One concept that may be helpful to you while considering a career in education is the image of a student teacher. Since you may already be a teacher of sorts for some of your friends, your siblings, and even adults or your parents, you should increase your awareness of your ability to convey your knowledge, skills, and interests to others. The concept of student teacher is based on a philosophy that describes people as being in a continual state of learning and teaching. In fact, even as a seasoned teacher, you will be constantly learning about new technologies, cultures, and teaching techniques. If you adopt this view now, you will have a head start as you develop yourself over the course of your lifetime of learning and sharing.

No matter what your background, interests, learning abilities, physical abilities, economic position, or geographic location is, you should feel empowered by the prospect of becoming a teacher. Regardless of who you are, you will have something important and unique to bring to the field. You can learn a lot about yourself and the world through teaching. A career in education is within your grasp.

METHODOLOGY OF THIS BOOK

One quick note before we begin. This book will ask you to imagine, brainstorm, take notes, and discuss your thoughts with your peers and others around you. It will ask you to act and think for yourself, just as a good teacher encourages you to do your own work. Education is always self-directed, and you are in the process of educating yourself about teaching. Because you are a unique individual, you will need to carve your own path. This book is not a script for you to follow. In a sense, you should be writing your own book as you go along.

The exercises suggested on the following pages need not take a lot of time. Even a few notes jotted down can be valuable. A couple of suggested discussions with teachers can provide lots of good ideas and insights. The goal of this book is to empower you and to make you an active factor in your own future. Skills, as well as knowledge, will be necessary as you determine your own career path.

Be sure to enjoy yourself as you explore the possibilities involved with becoming a teacher!

CHAPTER 2

WHAT YOU CAN DO TO START TODAY

At this point, a career in education should be one of a number of careers you are considering. This chapter is intended to help you start thinking about teaching. In fact, you can start on your path toward becoming a teacher today. All it takes is a change of perspective and an awareness of yourself, your school, and the various roles at your school. You can start thinking of parts of your personal and school lives as steps toward building a successful career as a teacher. All of the elements for starting this process of brainstorming are available to you right now. This chapter will help you ask and answer questions in order to take advantage of the important and useful information that is all around you, especially at school.

A FRESH PERSPECTIVE

Imagine you put on a pair of magic glasses. With these glasses, everything takes on a new light. Suddenly, you see the world from the perspective of a teacher. Isn't this the opposite perspective of what you have experienced up until now as a student? Looking through the eyes of a teacher can make school look very different.

But now that you have those glasses on, what do you see? Ask yourself questions from the perspective of a teacher. What are teachers' days like? When do they get up in the morning? Who are their bosses? How do teachers of different subjects differ from one another? Brainstorm on more questions like these, and scribble down some answers. Starting to consider school from the teacher's perspective is the first step you can take in preparing for your career as a teacher.

Obviously, considering things from a teacher's perspective is going to require some change. As a student, your emphasis is on your own success. From a teacher's perspective, you have to think about the success of others. Teachers succeed by helping others succeed. For example, in some situations teachers need to help their students conduct their own discussions to develop their own ideas. Effective teachers know how to bring out the best in their students. It can be enlightening to realize that sometimes the best teachers do not hold doctor of philosophy degrees (Ph.D.s) in their field but are nonetheless extremely effective educators. A good teacher has both types of knowledge—knowledge of the subject area (math, science, etc.) and knowledge of how to work with students by creating environments and situations through which students can learn and grow.

So far in this chapter we have begun thinking about, observing, and imagining the lives of teachers. But this is just the beginning. Now it is time to start making some decisions and guiding your current and future experiences toward becoming a teacher. If you are considering a career in teaching, there are a variety of things you can do, even before you graduate from high school. This chapter will help you brainstorm some ideas. What can you do to find out if teaching is for you? What can you do to simulate the experience of being a teacher? How can you start building a résumé that will help get you into college and into that first job? Actually, the skills, techniques, and knowledge presented in this chapter will be critical whether you pursue a career in education or some other field.

THINGS YOU CAN DO AT YOUR OWN SCHOOL

Undoubtedly, your own school is the best place to start when considering a career as a teacher. You understand your school and your teachers better than anyone from the outside ever could. Just like a fingerprint, schools are unique but share characteristics with millions of others. Part of what you might realize is that schools are shaped by their individual parts—that is, by their teachers and the administration. Take advantage of opportunities to observe and learn from these various role players. We will explore possibilities for building relationships with teachers on a more adult level later in this chapter. But for now, let's look at what you can do as a regular student at your school to start on a path toward teaching.

TUTORING

Tutoring is a natural way to start developing yourself as a teacher. As you grow older, you gain experience, knowledge, and skills that you may wish to share with others. Tutors can help younger children but may also be able to tutor those of the same age or even older people. Tutors can help in a variety of ways, for instance, by answering questions, helping with homework, and assisting with larger projects. But tutors may also help others with their study and organizational skills, for example, by showing how to keep an assignment book or how to manage time effectively while taking on large loads of work.

Tutoring can occur on a volunteer basis, but it could also turn into part-time work. One of the great things about tutoring is that it involves a one-on-one situation. Finding a quiet place for focused study can be a great first step in helping someone overcome confusion or frustration with their homework. As you tutor, take special note of the assignments given. Try to put yourself in the teacher's shoes, thinking about what the point of the assigned home-work is, what it is trying to accomplish, and so on. In this fashion, you will be able to indirectly observe many teach-ers' ways of teaching. You can learn a lot from tutoring with regard to teaching.

FINDING A MENTOR

A mentor is a person with ample experience who is available to you as a resource. Of course, almost anyone can help with advice no matter his or her age or profes-sion. But as you think more seriously about becoming an educator, consider building a relationship with a teacher at your school. Ideally, this will be someone you relate to, someone who reminds you of yourself, some-one you respect, and someone who has time for you. At the very least, schedule a five- or ten-minute meeting to let your teacher know you've been thinking about a career in teaching. Ask some basic questions, such as, How long have you been teaching? What do you enjoy about teaching? What don't you like about teaching? What kinds of qualities do you think teachers should have? What degrees did you earn before becoming a teacher? You're almost sure to discover that teachers are very encouraging and excited to talk to students who are considering a career in education.

If possible, explore ideas for a project or activity you might share with your mentor. See if you can assist with some of his or her administrative tasks, such as organiz-ing class notes, making photocopies, or looking through textbooks for extra problem sets. You might use your mentor as a faculty sponsor for a new club or program.

ACCESSING RESOURCES

THE LIBRARY

Your own school library can be a convenient and useful resource as you try to understand more about the world of teaching. Specifically, high school libraries contain information on a variety of vocational and educational opportunities. Whole series of books are available that describe various careers. Check out a few and compare things such as lifestyle, salary, necessary skills, and educational requirements. The Internet will be explored more fully later in this chapter, but for now, realize that libraries often provide free access to this useful resource.

Indeed, your librarian can be a key supporter of your research and career exploration. Introduce yourself as someone who is looking into career opportunities—in particular ones in education. Your librarian will undoubtedly have ideas for relevant resources, both within and outside of the school library. If you build a presence for yourself in the library, your librarian will keep you in mind and may start to set aside articles, journals, books, and other materials for you to review.

COLLEGE AND CAREER COUNSELOR

Make an appointment with your school's college and career counselor to discuss some of the ideas for careers you have been considering. The career and college office may have its own library with catalogs and listings of relevant programs. One of the first goals should be making a list of college programs that interest you (refer to the For More Information section for a listing of education programs nationwide). Have the counselor tell you about former students from your school who have had similar interests, and ask what careers they got involved with after college. You might also ask about your counselor's own experience with education. In fact, your counselor may be a prime candidate for becoming a special mentor at your very own school.

College programs will be discussed in chapter 8 of this book. After you read through that chapter, discuss the variety of college programs with your counselor. Review the ways you can highlight your experiences and your accomplishments in order to eventually submit an outstanding college application. Your counselor will help you develop a checklist for what you will need before you apply, including test scores, teacher recommendations, and transcripts. Schedule a follow-up meeting to discuss your progress, review the materials you have gathered, and track your ideas.

YOUR SCHOOL'S PRINCIPAL OR HEADMASTER

Your school principal or headmaster is not just there for when a student gets into trouble. In fact, heads of schools would prefer having discussions with students that are positive and looking toward the future. Many administrators started off just like you, with education as one of many options. Ask your principal about his or her own history and relationship with education. What subject did he or she teach? Where? What college degrees does he or she hold? Returning to the present, you might ask, What are some of the responsibilities of a head of school? What are some of the benefits of being a school administrator? You might even turn your interview into an article for the school newspaper. You might be surprised to find out how accessible your principal actually is. Principals and other heads of schools have devoted their lives to education.

Your Fellow Students

Interestingly, the students around you on the bus, at lunch, and in your clubs represent a resource for you as you consider teaching. Of course, your friends can give you more in-depth information, but you can learn even from those you don't know very well. Listen to what they say. For example, what do they complain about? What teachers do they like or dislike? What would they want to change at school? Also, notice how students behave in different situations. How will the same student change his or her behavior in different situations, from during to after school, around different people, in front of teachers, and so on? What issues are on students' minds?

Students have a great deal of influence on the learning environment. Good teachers take advantage of the characteristics of different student groups in order to maximize learning and participation. Effective teachers keep in mind what it is like to be a young person or a teenager so they can relate to their students. For you, too, any notes or memories you can hold on to now will greatly help you when you become a teacher. Using this perspective can help you motivate, guide, and focus members of your future classes. Of course, teachers hold on to their understanding of what it is to be a student because many of them are still students in graduate programs or are taking other classes.

Things You Can Do Outside of School

Obviously, school is a place where you can observe and learn a lot on your way toward becoming a teacher. However, the time you spend away from school—including afternoons, weekends, vacations, and summers—allows you to work on your own activities and hobbies as well as to share time with people you enjoy. Through all these experiences, you are really discovering opportunities for important learning and growth. In fact, these activities and exercises will eventually prove to be central as you develop your career. Personal relationships, sports, and creative endeavors all factor into who you are and who you will become as an adult. With an open mind, you can turn the things you love into valuable and relevant experiences that will shape your professional career as well.

EXTRACURRICULAR ACTIVITIES

The possibilities for after-school and weekend activities are infinite. Among the millions of high school students in the United States, no two have exactly the same interests and hobbies.

A number of activities seem particularly relevant to building skills as a teacher. Animal care remains a classic way of caring for others and promoting others' development. Taking care of animals requires a strong commitment and consideration for the well-being of the pet. Assisting a young children's sports team would help you gain insight into how it feels to have a group rely on you for support, guidance, and protection. Think of other activities that relate directly to the skills of creating goals, motivating, and organizing others.

Most certainly, taking lessons represents another type of experience in which you are in contact with a teacher. Whether you take lessons in music, dance, sports, or academic subjects, your commitment to the lessons will help you understand what it takes to accomplish goals as an individual or as part of a team. You will witness first-hand the way a teacher or tutor structures a series of lessons, creates an environment in which the lessons can be successful, gains your respect, and maximizes your performance at whatever you are doing.

The study of language in an extracurricular class includes experiences that will become useful later on when you come into contact with students representing unfamiliar cultures—something you will undoubtedly experience as a teacher. Communication across cultural lines through the study of customs, idioms, and religious beliefs will strengthen your ability to overcome difficult situations in teaching where barriers can also include age, socioeconomic, and philosophical differences.

If you are concerned with your scores on college board examinations like the SAT, try taking an extracurricular course that aims to improve your score. Test preparation courses are another opportunity to learn about teaching while accomplishing other goals. Pay close attention to the way your instructor delivers material, uses textbooks and other resources, and evaluates your improvement over time.

COMMUNITY SERVICE

Performing community service relates to teaching and education in a number of important ways. First and foremost is the element of giving back to your community in a selfless fashion. By doing community service, you are asking not how you can succeed personally but how you can assist others as they overcome obstacles. This is very similar to the world of education. The types of service you can perform are unlimited, from building new structures to clearing old structures, and from making a meal for someone to sharing a meal with someone. As you gain experience with community service, you will find yourself increasingly in leadership roles and coordinating groups with the goal of bettering communities. Notably, the concept of community is an important one for schools because schools create communities within their own walls. The school's community can even be seen as a meeting place for members of different outside communities. Teachers are key role-players who help their school communities work.

Another example of community service is working with the disabled. This can be a challenging and rewarding experience. Because disabilities can be physical and/or mental and range in severity, understanding the capabilities of the people you work with becomes an important skill. Every person has his or her strengths and weaknesses, but people with more severe disabilities need to be encouraged in what they can do so they can overcome what they cannot. This is a fabulous way for you to motivate others and to realize and accomplish goals. The bonds, friendships, and camaraderie involved in working with disabled people may just prove to be the most memorable and touching experience of your life. It can give you a taste of the satisfaction and intangible rewards of teaching as a profession.

BUILDING CONNECTIONS AND A NETWORK

Sometimes, it can be easier to have conversations with people in your personal life than with adults at school. In this spirit, ask older members in your family if they have any acquaintances or relatives working in education. Finding a mentor outside of your own school can help you avoid uncomfortable tension with competitive classmates or other peer pressures at school. Meet with your connections and tell them about yourself. Ask questions, request ideas, and find out about other leads you might pursue that will help you learn more about a career in education. Be sure to express your own goals and position in your career search.

By combining the knowledge and advice from your contacts outside of school with the resources you are accessing within your school, you can build a powerful team that can help you get into the college program of your choice and secure interviews for work opportunities starting immediately. Don't be reluctant to let other people help you because accomplishments are usually made through joint efforts. Most times, you will find it extremely difficult to achieve any of this on your own, so don't forget to give credit and thanks where they are due.

CULTIVATE YOURSELF AND YOUR INTERESTS

Although some people feel most comfortable at school, studying, and doing schoolwork, many of us identify more with outside interests. The good news for you and your career as an educator is that your outside interests are essential as you acquire skills and knowledge. The ways you can apply your schoolwork to your interests and your interests to your schoolwork are infinite. Any talents you have developed, even if they are in alternative areas such as skateboarding or hip-hop music, will help define you at a number of points in your career: in applying to college, completing college credits, interviewing for jobs, creating lessons for your students, and so on. Your interests are what set you apart, make you memorable to prospective colleges and employers, and make you an intriguing individual. Your interests can bring you around the country and even around the world. Take mental notes on different individuals, communities, states, and countries that you experience. Your interests can put you into contact with new people and new experiences that open up doors, provide important contacts, and widen your understanding of the world—an important element to the modern teacher.

EXPLORING OTHER RESOURCES

With the increased prevalence of technology and the improvement of databases and listings, huge amounts of information are available to you. Although this information represents a valuable resource, sometimes an overabundance of information can be intimidating. This section will help you build your awareness and skill level with researching and gathering information. It will also give you some ideas for organizing the materials you compile. With an organized and informed approach, you can make research a snap! Fluency with these tools and competence in these skills are necessary when you are building any career or moving toward any goal.

THE INTERNET

The amount of information on the Internet has increased exponentially since the early 1990s. Just think, even as late as 1995, most people didn't have access to the Internet. It is estimated that by 2002, the online population in the United States alone had reached more than 200 million people. The typical Web surfer visited pages online an estimated average of more than ninety times per week! And some estimates reveal that the number of Web sites grew from 130 in 1993 to more than 50 million today. Needless to say, you could spend your entire life downloading and reading information made available to you on the Internet.

What is important is that you have to increase your knowledge of the Internet. No matter how much you think you know, there is always more to learn. These skills will remain invaluable to you throughout the process of becoming and succeeding as a teacher. You must be able to use a search engine, sift through thousands of search results, scan articles to find relevant and authoritative information, copy and paste important passages into a word-processing document, and label your information with the Web site address so that it can be found again later. Familiarity with shortcuts and functions within your browser will further expedite your research. For those of you with your own computers or with server space reserved through your school, another essential skill involves keeping your computer files organized and labeled for easy use.

EDUCATIONAL WEB SITES

Branches of state, city, county, and the federal government offer Web sites for educators and students looking to become teachers. Choose any town, state, or county and do a search on its board of education. There you will find information on what jobs are available, areas of severe demand, special programs seeking to attract teachers, and dates of job fairs aimed directly at people like you. Credential, licensing, and testing information may also be available on these Web sites.

Don't forget that commercial Web sites can be important sources of information, too. In particular, sites that specialize in books can offer the fastest access to pertinent sources. The catalog listings for some commercial Web sites can be broader and more up-to-date than library collections. Also, these sites provide listings of books with similar content and by the same author. If you're interested in a particular book, you can use a commercial Web site to find competing publishers' books that contain related information. You can also search by subject area to obtain a list of similar books.

COLLEGE CATALOGS AND PROGRAM MATERIALS

Colleges invariably have massive amounts of information posted online. Course catalogs are updated every semester but can be cryptic and difficult to understand. Instead, look for pages with general information on entire programs, such as departments within undergraduate programs, or graduate schools of education. These sites will list requirements for mandatory tests, courses, and student teaching hours. Check out some of these sites to start getting a sense for what a college or certification program will entail. Keep in mind that colleges prefer to save on costs of printing by making their materials available online. Some college applications can even be completed online. College Web sites further offer the opportunity to ask direct questions through e-mail or other Web forms. To find online resources for a college or certification program, go to a search engine and type in the name of the college. Once at the college's Web site, look for its school of education to learn more about what programs the college offers.

You can also request college catalogs and program materials directly from the school or program. These can be requested in a number of different ways—by mail, by phone, and through the Internet. Colleges make available applications, teacher certification information, bulletins, and newsletters that can describe the experience of their programs as well as requirements for acceptance and course completion.

STATE AGENCIES AND DEPARTMENTS

Likewise, online search engines can lead you to state departments of education. Go to a search engine and type in the name of the state followed by the words "state department of education." States take on much of the responsibility for overseeing budgeting, setting standards for curricula, pursuing legal resolutions to litigation, compiling statistics, and determining requirements for teacher certification. Certain states are in dire need of teachers in certain subject areas and will let you know through advertisements on their Web sites. States run a number of different programs for students of all ages, including special education, early start programs, and grants for schools and school districts. States are also boosting the presence of technology such as computers in schools in order to prepare their students for careers in today's economy. School calendars, special reports, relevant Web links, recently passed legislation, and other news can be found on these department of education Web sites.

GRANTS

A grant is any monetary aid given out by public or private organizations. Most grants have strict guidelines and application processes. Grants that you could explore involve receiving aid in the form of money, scholarships,

California Department of
EDUCATION

| Home | | Curriculum & Instruction | Testing & Accountability | Professional Development |
| Superintendent | | Finance & Grants | Data & Statistics | Learning Support | Specialized Programs |

- • Vision & Mission
- • Offices
- • Newsroom

Board of Education
- • Standards & Frameworks
- • Meeting Agendas
- • Members & Staff

Our Vision

To create a dynamic, world-class education system that equips all students with the knowledge and skills to excel in college and careers, and excel as parents and citizens.

**Superintendent
Jack O'Connell**

What's new

Press Packet - 2004 API/AYP Guide
Posted 25-Aug-2004

State Superintendent's High School Summit 2004
Posted 19-Aug-2004

2004 STAR Results
Posted 18-Aug-2004

more...

Highlights

No Child Left Behind
California's homepage for the No Child Left Behind Act of 2001 (NCLB) serves as a clearinghouse for information on California's ongoing implementation of NCLB.

Academic Performance Index (API)
The cornerstone of the California's Public Schools Accountability Act of 1999 (PSAA), measures the academic performance and growth of schools.

Standardized Testing and Reporting (STAR)
The STAR program is to help measure how well students are learning basic academic skills.

Resources

- ■ Calendars
- ■ Department Information
- ■ Equal Opportunity and Access
- ■ Funding Opportunities
- ■ Laws & Regulations
- ■ Publications
- ■ School Directory
- ■ Staff Directory
- ■ Web Site-Table of Contents

more...

California Department of Education
1430 N Street
Sacramento, CA 95814

Contact Us | Web Policy | Feedback

Last Modified: Wednesday, August 25, 2004

Each state's department of education offers a Web site with information regarding standards and curriculum, directories, and laws and regulations. At these Web sites, you can also learn about grants and other opportunities available.

access to resources for research, and job opportunities. Grants are available for unlimited demographic groups and for unlimited purposes. It has been estimated that in 2003, there were more than 1,400 federal programs, 24,000 state programs, 30,000 private foundations, and 20,000 scholarship programs available. Education is one of the most common areas in which grants are awarded. Usually, a grant is established with a specific purpose, and applicants present themselves as fitting within that purpose. If you are awarded a grant, you will be responsible for reporting back and showing that you have fulfilled the aims of the grant.

Of course, the Internet is a primary tool for finding grant listings. Check departments of education, including the federal government's U.S. Department of Education. Public libraries are another source. There are numerous guides to grants listed by the federal government that are available online or at bookstores. Various books are available to help you build your grant-writing skills as well. Obviously, grant money is something that isn't going to come knocking at your door. The money is out there, but you have to put some effort into researching and applying for these funds—and it is worth it!

PUBLIC LIBRARIES

You might be surprised at how accessible the information housed in public libraries can be. Plus, you don't even have to travel to most libraries, since it has become economical and efficient for libraries to list their collections online. This means that you can search for books, check availability, and obtain catalog numbers for books from any Internet connection. Libraries can also be a convenient place to get free Internet access.

Many libraries take career hunting very seriously. There are usually distinct sections of the library devoted to providing resources to people looking into new careers—people just like you. Some of their collections may be "reference only," which means that you cannot take the books home, but you may read and photocopy them in the library.

STARTING TO THINK ABOUT COLLEGE APPLICATIONS

College applications are not as difficult as you might think, especially if you start preparing for them now. Even if you are not a senior in high school, request a copy of a college application just to see what kinds of things you will need to submit. From this, you will learn how long your essay is supposed to be, how many teacher recommendations you need, and what standardized test scores are required. Some applications ask for information about any special achievements or awards you have received. Find out about the awards offered at your school and determine those that are within your reach.

Some college applications want you to include peer recommendations; they ask you to find classmates who will describe your school life in a positive light. Being aware of these required materials now can help you set up good relationships that have a goal in mind. For example, wouldn't it be better to approach a teacher a few months ahead of time to ask that he or she observe you in preparation for writing a recommendation, rather than disturbing the teacher at the last minute with a desperate request? By asking early, you will be able to discuss how you can improve your performance in order to help that teacher write a glowing recommendation.

CHAPTER 3

THE WIDE ARRAY OF OPPORTUNITIES IN TEACHING

Diversity is a prevalent concept in the world of education. In fact, the great diversity of the North American population is reflected directly in students today. All around North America, students represent a variety of distinct cultures and diversity often broken down according to language, economic class, race, culture, and religion. This wide array of people is being educated in a variety of ways. As such, generalizing about schools in the United States becomes a very difficult task. However, as this chapter will show, there are a few ways to organize teachers into groups— for example, by grouping teachers into those in private and public schools. This chapter will allow you to explore, compare, and contrast the variety of options you have available to you as a prospective teacher.

PUBLIC VS. PRIVATE SCHOOL TEACHING

Most students should be aware of the basic differences between public and private schools, and how to identify them. One main difference between public and private schools is their source of funding. Public institutions are those supported by federal, state, and local governments. In the United States, all students—regardless of gender, race, culture, and ability—are guaranteed the right to a free appropriate public education (FAPE) provided by the state. Public schools represent the way government departments of education offer these services to the majority of the citizens of the country. Conversely, private schools are funded privately by parents of students, alumni, and other supporters. So, although public schools are guaranteed and even required by the government, private schools are used voluntarily by parents who seek an alternative education for their children.

High school students sometimes do not realize that the public/private school distinction is something that reaches into the college level. Public colleges are usually considerably less expensive than private colleges, primarily because they are supported and taxed differently by the state agencies that govern them.

A number of sources for statistics are available regarding education in the United States. Of them, the National Center for Education Statistics (NCES), using figures from the U.S. Census Bureau, provides some of the most comprehensive and useful information. The NCES estimates that public schools account for some 90 percent of all elementary and secondary school students, with private schools educating the remaining 10 percent. Both the Census Bureau and the number crunchers at the NCES estimate that the student-age population by the year 2013 will grow by 11 percent in public schools and 18 percent in private schools. This follows a boom in students from the years 1987 to 2001 in both categories as well. This is good news for those young people wishing to become teachers: when the number of students rises, there will be an increased demand for teachers in both the public and private sectors. More in-depth information about the changing demand for teachers will be given later in this book.

Funding may be the main difference between public and private schools, but there is a lot more to it. Let's take a look at the basic differences between these types of schools. Of course, all public schools are not alike, and private schools can also vary considerably in a number of ways. But you should understand how public schools differ from private schools, and how there are differences within each category. The experience is not only different for the student but for the teacher as well.

PUBLIC SCHOOLS

Sure, public schools are publicly funded, but do you know how? The way public schools are funded will become more important to you when you become a teacher, for a number of reasons. Every school has a budget, or a dollar amount it can use, which allows it to operate, purchase materials, and maintain its facilities. School budgets come out of larger budgets, most often from their school districts, which are groups of schools within a single geographic area. School districts are mostly funded from the taxes of business and homeowners living in that geographic area. People who own their own houses, apartments, and commercial properties pay what is called property tax.

The funding intricacies have consequences for how public schools operate. For example, school budgets can vary greatly from region to region, from state to state, and even from community to community. Look at a large city like Chicago. Some of the public schools in Chicago appear clean, safe, and filled with students eager to move on to top college programs. However, other public schools in the city are in need of repairs, have security checkpoints at their entrances, and have students who attend class only because it is required by law. Schools are the products of their communities. If the community does not support its schools by devoting tax money, raising additional money, and contributing in other ways, the schools will suffer, and ultimately, the community will suffer.

Some schools benefit from the support of parent organizations, booster clubs, and concerned school district administrations that fight to attract money from the government and other sources. Schools that are supported by concerned and dedicated individuals produce observable results that benefit students. Although some people point out flaws in the U.S. public school system, some of the best educational facilities in the nation are public schools, producing academic award winners, students accepted into the finest colleges, and leaders of their generations.

Many parents know which communities have good schools and will often move so their children can attend them. Conversely, people or businesses who have no interest in high-quality schools will avoid areas that have high property taxes. The problem with this system is that many students are stuck in public schools that are underfunded and neglected by their communities and their representatives in local and state governments.

Federal, state, and city governments are aware of this and have designed programs to attract human and financial resources to these schools. As a young teacher, these programs can work to your advantage if you decide to pursue a career in the public school system. These programs often offer competitive salaries, special cash awards, and subsidized college credits to people who agree to work in disadvantaged public schools, both in rural and urban areas.

As a public school teacher, you will have a great deal of control in deciding the schools in which you teach, but in some cases not complete control. Once you have received a certificate to teach, you will be able to apply for jobs all over the country, and even all over the world. You can research the quality of schools in communities and apply for jobs in areas that interest you.

In some cases, as with large cities, you may not have as much control over your working conditions. As mentioned previously, the quality of schools in large metropolitan areas can vary greatly, and once you are hired by a city department of education, you may be transferred involuntarily to a school that is farther away from where you live or that is otherwise undesirable for you. This is more likely to happen if you are a teacher in a subject that is in great demand. So, before you commit to employing yourself with a large board of education, be sure to research information concerning your ability to select and transfer between schools.

It is difficult to generalize about the conditions that will greet you as a public school teacher. However, many teachers experience some distinctive characteristics in public schools. In general, budgets restrict luxuries such as available offices and equipment, faculty lounges, access to telephones and the Internet, and other perks that are present in other careers. Required hours can vary—work hours generally decrease as the grade level being taught increases. Elementary school teachers work very long hours, while high school teachers may be able to take on extra work after school, perhaps tutoring or running an after-school program at a separate location.

Generally, a public school teacher's workday runs from about 8:30 AM to 3 PM. To prepare for their classes, teachers need time for lesson planning, which requires the creation of handouts, lectures, and test materials. Lesson planning time is valued and incorporated into teachers' weekly schedules. High school teachers may be offered one preparation period, one lunch period, and one professional period in addition to five periods of classes daily. Elementary school teachers receive one daily preparation period and one lunch period. Class sizes at public high schools are generally twenty-five to thirty-five students; elementary schools average between twenty and thirty students per class. Regular teachers may be asked to carry out some additional responsibilities, such as supervising lunch or playground areas. Public school teachers are not required to help organize after-school activities.

CLASS SIZES IN PUBLIC SCHOOLS

Class size is a hot topic for public school teachers. Research and anecdotal evidence show that students respond to smaller class sizes and individualized attention. In 2001, the U.S. government passed legislation called, with some fanfare, the No Child Left Behind Act. This act allows states and local education agencies to use federal funds to hire qualified teachers. The federal government has reported that school districts received billions of dollars for the recruitment and training of

Problems	Percent																		
	1970	1975	1980	1985	1988	1989	1990	1991	1992	1993	1994	1995	1996	1997	1998	1999	2000	2001	2002
1	2	3	4	5	6	7	8	9	10	11	12	13	14	15	16	17	18	19	20
Lack of discipline	18	23	26	25	19	19	19	20	17	15	18	15	15	15	14	18	15	15	17
Lack of financial support	17	14	10	9	12	13	13	18	22	21	13	11	13	15	12	9	18	15	23
Fighting/violence/gangs	---	---	---	---	---	---	---	9	13	18	9	14	12	15	11	11	10	9	
Use of drugs	11	9	14	18	32	34	38	22	22	16	11	7	16	14	10	8	9	9	13
Standards/quality of education	---	---									8	4	---	8	6	2	5	---	---
Large schools/overcrowding	---	10	7	5	6	8	7	9	9	8	7	3	8	8	8	8	12	10	17
Lack of respect	---	---	---	---	---	---	---	---			3	3	2	---	2	2	2	---	---
Lack of family structure/ problems of home life	---	---	---	---	---	---	---	---			5	3	4	---	---	---	---	---	---
Crime/vandalism	---	---	---	---	---	---	---	---			4	2	3	---	2	5	5	---	---
Getting good teachers	12	11	6	10	11	7	7	11	5	5	3	2	3	3	5	4	4	6	8
Parents' lack of interest	3	2	6	3	7	6	4	7	5	4	3	2	---	---	2	4	4	---	---
Pupils' lack of interest/truancy	---	3	5	5	5	3	6	10	9	5	4	3	2	5	6	5	2	---	---
Integration/segregation/ racial discrimination	17	15	10	4	4	4	5	5	4	4	3	2	2	---	---	---	---	---	---
Management of funds/programs	---	---	---	---	---	---	---	---	---	---		2	---	---	---	---	---	---	---
Moral standards	---	---	---	2	6	3	3	3	4	3	---	---	---	---	2	2	---	---	---
Low teacher pay	---	---	---	2	4	4	6	4	3	3	---	---	---	---	2	2	4	---	---
Teachers' lack of interest	6	5	11	11	11	8	8	10	9	9	3	2	3	---	1	2	2	---	---
Drinking/alcoholism	---	---	2	3	5	4	4	2	2	---	---	---	---	---	---	---	---	---	---
Lack of proper facilities	11	3	2	1	1	1	2	---	---	---	---	---	---	---	---	---	---	---	---

---Not available.

SOURCE: Phi Delta Kappa, Phi Delta Kappan "The Annual Gallup Poll of the Public's Attitudes Toward the Public Schools," various years. (This table was prepared August 2002.)

The table above shows the results of a survey in 2002 in which parents were asked what was the biggest problem with the schools in their communities. According to this survey, lack of funding was the number one problem. Overcrowding and a lack of discipline tied as the second biggest problems.

30,000 new teachers for the 2001 to 2002 school year. Acting on their own initiative, states such as California have aggressively sought to provide funds for schools to hire extra teachers and create classroom space, enabling smaller class sizes. Clearly the reduction of class size is a priority for public education in the new millennium.

UNIONS

Teachers' unions, which also support smaller class sizes, are an aspect of public school teaching that can shape a teacher's experiences in a number of ways. Unions present themselves as advocates not only for teachers but also for students, arguing that improved school conditions benefit both parties. By representing a wide range of participants in education, unions gain support, strength, and influence. Their membership can include teachers, paraprofessionals, school secretaries, guidance counselors, psychologists, social workers, education evaluators, nurses, laboratory technicians, adult education teachers, and retired members. Unions aim to make schools places where students want to learn and teachers want to teach. Unions can help attract and retain high-quality educators who understand what conditions they require to be productive and satisfied at work.

Unions elect officials that negotiate directly with the board of education or school district to maintain competitive salaries and acceptable working conditions for teachers. Unions also work toward creating safer, more orderly schools, improving school facilities, and increasing parent involvement in schools. However, along with unions comes the possibility of strikes. Days off spent striking are not paid. Also, teachers who belong to unions must pay dues that average about $500 annually. Despite the fact that joining a teachers' union is optional, about half of the public school teachers in the United States are members of at least one union. Two large national unions that you might check out are the American Federation of Teachers and the National Education Association.

BENEFITS AND PUBLIC SCHOOLS

Among the benefits of being a public school teacher is one that is actually called benefits. In this sense of the word, benefits are extra incentives that are written into the teacher's contract along with the salary. Because the benefits offered to public school teachers are appealing, these perks can be as important or even more important than salary for some people.

So what do these benefits include? First and foremost is health insurance. Many industrialized countries provide socialized medicine, meaning that their citizens pay a tax and are provided with medical services when necessary. However, in the United States, citizens must secure their own health care. With the rising costs associated with medical care and insurance today, many people regard employer-subsidized health benefits as important. Teachers usually qualify for attractive and comprehensive health insurance programs because they are employees of the state. Since state insurance programs are very large, this allows each member to pay only a small amount each month. Such programs can pool enough funds for those in need. Therefore, public school systems can afford to offer low-cost health insurance not only for the teacher but also for his or her entire family. This can save families hundreds of dollars per month, and thousands per year.

Another benefit included in public teacher contracts involves paid leave. Teachers are granted a number of paid days off each year, so they still receive their salary when they are out sick, have a family emergency, are called to jury duty, or just feel they need a well-deserved day off.

Retirement programs represent another kind of benefit. As with health insurance, teachers qualify for statewide retirement programs that pool massive amounts of money into pension funds. These funds can make money for those who retire. Oftentimes, retired public school teachers receive monthly checks that equal or surpass the amounts they earned when they were still working. Most retirement benefits can be transferred to other states, and state retirement funds are very stable and insured by the government. Private companies and private schools may not be able to insure their retirement and other benefits as well as the state can because they could go bankrupt someday.

And, of course, a major benefit for teachers is vacation time. Educators have some of the longest and most frequent vacations compared to people in other careers. Summer break, winter break, spring break—it all adds up to a lot of paid vacation time.

Although salaries for public school teachers can be notoriously low when compared with other careers, the teachers receive benefit packages that remain highly competitive. The plenitude of teacher's benefits should be reason enough to seriously consider a career in public education.

PRIVATE SCHOOLS

Think about what the word "private" means. You might associate it with concepts like "privacy," but the "private" in private schools is more like the "private" in private property, which is the opposite of public property. Properties or entities that are held privately are owned and managed by individuals who have control over their use. So, private schools are simply businesses that provide a service for people seeking a specific educational experience. As you will see, there are many differences between working at a public school and a private school.

Tuition (the cost of attending the school) at private schools can be very high and usually increases every year. However, private schools cannot pay all of their bills using tuition money alone. Turning to alumni and other benefactors for support, private schools are able to raise and invest pools of money just like other private businesses do. Private schools, like some public schools, have boards of trustees who are in charge of hiring and firing the school administration and making other important decisions affecting the school. Unlike with public schools, the hierarchy of the people who run a private school is relatively simple, with bureaucracy kept to a minimum. This just means that private schools have less people on salary and can be more efficient with the money they have available. Dollar for dollar, private schools usually apply more money to the actual education of their students than public schools do.

A number of important implications rise out of the fact that private schools are relatively independent from government control. For example, the government cannot require private school students to take any standardized tests, nor can they enforce any state-decreed curriculum. Also, private schools are not held to any standards in terms of the teachers they hire. Private schools can hire teachers without state certification and even without any formal training in education. Therefore, teachers at private schools often have more actual experience in their fields of study because they may have worked non-teaching jobs for a number of years. Teachers coming from other professions may at first have less knowledge of regular teaching skills, but they are highly valued because of their expertise.

In addition, private schools differ from public schools in that they can incorporate religion into their mission statements, classes, and weekly schedules. Another aspect of this independence from government standards means that private school teachers are free to develop their own curricula and choose their own textbooks without concern for state requirements and tests.

Private school teachers can benefit from the improved quality of their schools in many ways. Their classrooms are more orderly and focused because of the smaller class sizes and generally because the students are more disciplined. Students in private schools may behave more maturely because they face expulsion for inappropriate behavior or lack of effort. In this fashion, students are held accountable for their actions. Classroom environments in private schools benefit from the combination of teachers with more expertise, students who are driven, modern facilities, and higher quality of class materials such as audiovisual equipment, computers, and books. Despite the fact that teacher's salaries and benefits are considerably more substantial at public schools, conditions at private schools are more conducive to positive experiences, both for the teacher and student. Therefore, positions at these schools remain attractive.

Private schools can vary greatly in quality, size, location, and philosophy. In some cases, parents choose private schools for their ability to socialize their students and to instill a specific set of cultural norms in their children. For instance, Japanese parents in San Francisco may want their sons or daughters to be familiar with Japanese language and customs, so they may choose a private Japanese American school. Some parents value religion, as with Christian parents who would look for schools that have mandatory worship services or Bible study classes as part of the required curriculum. Boarding schools in the Northeast comprise another distinctive group that is typically characterized by dress code, long-standing traditions, and students who live away from home beginning at a relatively early age. Students may also have intense interests in sports or other activities that help them decide to attend schools that emphasize these areas. Some private schools have students that come from all over the country and all over the world.

RELIGIOUS SCHOOLS

Religious schools are private schools affiliated with religious organizations, including those of the Jewish, Islamic, and

Christian faiths. Catholic schools are the most common of the religous schools in the United States. Catholic schools resemble private schools in most respects, including the fact that they educate students of all types and religions. Although some groups report that the number of Catholic schools and their graduates is increasing, others show a decline in their numbers. When compared with public schools and nonreligious private schools, salaries may be lower at Catholic or other religious schools. Notably, when applying to work as a teacher at a religious school, you may be required to submit a statement describing your relationship with religion. Qualifications necessary to teach at a religious school will vary from school to school.

SPECIAL EDUCATION VS. REGULAR EDUCATION

The field of special education has grown through the efforts of parents, educators, lobbyists, and legislators in federal and state governments. In the beginning of the twentieth century, children with observable disabilities were excluded from regular school programs. During the last century, attitudes have shifted from regarding these students as "retarded" to seeing them as "special," and most recently as "exceptional." Essentially, the U.S. government has gone through a similar process of recognizing all students, regardless of ability or disability, as eligible for the free appropriate public education required for all American citizens. According to the Individuals with Disabilities Education Act (IDEA) of 1990, public school districts are required to educate and provide services to those students who have special needs, regardless of the cost. A number of lawsuits between students with severe needs and poorly funded school districts have followed the passage of this legislation.

In the meantime, the federal government has begun to define individual groups and provide guidelines for the services that should be provided by schools. The deaf, the blind, and those with other severe physical conditions are considered eligible for special services and facilities despite the fact that these students intellectually resemble regular students. Other conditions include mental retardation, autism, behavioral disorders, and cerebral palsy.

The group experiencing the highest level of growth and acknowledgment is called learning disabled. Students with learning disabilities include those with isolated difficulties in reading (such as dyslexia), writing (such as dysgraphia), and memory. Since students with learning disabilities have benefited from specialized instruction, whole schools have emerged to provide special services to these students.

In 2001, the U.S. Department of Education reported that learning disabilities represented the largest category of students receiving special education services with more than 2.8 million students. Learning disabilities represented approximately 50 percent of the special education population, in contrast with the next-largest category, speech and language impairments, comprising 19 percent. The third-largest category, mental retardation, represented about 11 percent of the total.

Inclusion is a concept that has recently emerged during the debate over how to educate students with special needs. Those in favor of inclusion demand that students remain in regular classrooms as much as possible, where they can develop relationships with "regular" students. Special services would be provided in the regular classroom to the greatest degree possible. Most often, a second teacher that has been trained in special education is placed in the classroom to assist with lesson planning, test development, and classroom management. In some cases, students with special needs are pulled out of the regular classroom for one or two class periods per day.

Inclusion has displaced the previous policy known as mainstreaming, under which students with special needs were kept separate from regular classrooms until they were deemed "ready" for regular instruction. Once the students returned to the regular classroom, or were "mainstreamed," they would receive no partial treatment. Inclusion requires teachers to take time to treat each student individually and to plan lessons that account for learning differences within the classroom. The rise of inclusion in America's public schools reveals the growing trend to move special education out of isolated rooms and into regular classrooms.

GROWING DEMAND IN SPECIAL ED

The demand for teachers with skills in special education has grown in proportion to the rise in the number of students being helped. Newspapers across the nation are filled with classified listings calling for teachers with certification and degrees in special education. Whereas special education used to be a broad category, various specializations have grown out of this field. Today, special education programs are broken down by age and type of disability. Teachers are trained in a variety of specialized skills that include observation of student behavior and performance, collection of data to quantify these observations, evaluations of disabilities, and the assessment of progress.

Individualized Education Plans, or IEPs, have become the standard format to indicate students' ability levels and their needs. IEP writing is yet another skill required of the special education teacher. Educators who have certification and experience with these skills are sought after, and schools are forced to offer competitive salaries in order to attract the people. Indeed, teachers in special education have a wide array of opportunities available to them across the country.

The conditions for teachers in special education are considerably different from those for regular teachers. Special education teachers perform a variety of tasks in their own classrooms, in other teachers' classrooms, or as consultants to other teachers. When pulling students out of their regular classrooms, special education teachers may end up working with a small group or even a single student. Because lessons must be customized for each student, state-mandated standardized tests are often not a concern. Therefore, special education teachers are able to design their own classes with more independence than do regular education teachers. Teachers working with the mentally retarded or others with severe learning disabilities must focus on an entirely different set of goals and skills for their students. What is most important for teaching special education is a positive outlook and a great deal of patience.

CHAPTER 4

DIFFERENT LEVELS OF EDUCATION

The experience of teaching children of different ages can vary dramatically. Although not every school system breaks its schools into the three levels—elementary, middle or junior high, and high school—this section will attempt to describe the distinctions you will experience while teaching different age groups. Schools are structured differently depending on the age of their students, so teachers will experience differences in work conditions, hours, preparation time, course content, skills being taught, and approaches to discipline in the classroom.

ELEMENTARY SCHOOL TEACHING

Think back on your first years in school. What do you think your teachers were trying to help you accomplish? If you recall your teacher settling fights on the playground, you will realize that instructing young children is about more than just teaching the alphabet or multiplication tables. Even though elementary school teachers formally introduce young children to academics, they are also addressing students' physical, emotional, and social development. Although the central focus in the elementary classroom remains reading, writing, and arithmetic, the teacher must guide students in a number of other areas: working in groups, getting along with classmates, respecting teachers and peers, caring for class materials, keeping track of personal belongings, and so on.

Have you heard of the book *Everything I Need to Know I Learned in Kindergarten*? As the title of this book implies, elementary teachers are asked to become role models, judges, and mentors to their students. Because of the wide age discrepancy, the difference between the teacher and the student is at its most extreme during these years. Elementary teachers stay with the same group of students for most of the day, every day of the school year. It is no wonder that some children become attached to, and in some cases idolize, their elementary school teachers, holding on to vivid, fond memories even into adulthood.

Of course, elementary school teachers should possess various attributes if they are to build the skills necessary for succeeding and enjoying their jobs year in and year out. Working with children requires an enormous amount of energy and positivity—praise works more effectively than scolding. Also, a love of play and a sense of humor help elementary school teachers win over the respect of their students. Teachers of young people know that children thrive when they clearly understand the rules and routines. With experience, elementary school teachers realize that they must embody structure and consistency to maintain this level of clarity in their classrooms. Teachers must understand the psychology of children to avoid conflict. Teachers of young children must also learn how to use discipline as a positive and effective tool. And above all, elementary school teachers must be creative with the use of academic and art materials to make lessons and the classroom environment as comfortable and conducive to learning as possible.

The conditions that elementary school teachers experience are different from teachers at other levels. Elementary school teachers work long hours, staying after school to meet with parents, reorganize their classrooms, attend meetings, and plan the next day's activities. Many elementary school classes are taught using a station method wherein students rotate from station to station in order to complete short assignments. Elementary school teachers may also work with assistants who help supervise these stations and assist with other tasks. Elementary school teachers are permitted few breaks since they are often asked to watch over their children during lunch and recess. Art, dance, or music classes taught by specialty teachers may offer the only chance for elementary school teachers to take a break, make personal phone calls, or perform last-minute class preparations. Since they teach their classes in a variety of different subjects, ranging from math to handwriting to science, elementary school teachers must truly be versatile, confident, and relaxed with all of the roles they must play over the course of a school day. Class sizes at public elementary schools are generally smaller than at other levels, averaging between twenty to thirty students each.

MIDDLE/JUNIOR HIGH SCHOOL TEACHING

When students arrive at middle school or junior high, they are accustomed to having teachers guide them through educational exercises to ensure success. For these students, each year of middle school represents a gradual step toward assuming more of their own responsibility and independence with regard to their academics.

Teaching middle-school-age children is distinctive for a number of reasons. With preteens, there can be a closeness and sense of family in the classroom that vanishes as students rebel and reject authority when they reach their teens. Middle school teachers enjoy observing their students transform themselves from children into young adults, a process that has physical, emotional, and intellectual aspects. Parents worry about their sons and daughters at this stage because mothers and fathers may be resistant to the changes occurring in their children's personal and academic lives. Teachers of middle school students are effective when they learn how to balance the delicate changing roles of their students' personal and academic lives.

Middle school teachers have distinctive schedules and responsibilities as well. Teachers of younger grades in middle schools, such as sixth and seventh grades, may resemble elementary school teachers because they are required to teach a variety of different subjects in any given day. By eighth grade, teachers may be able to stick to a single subject. So, with the younger students, middle school teachers have to prepare numerous lessons on a daily basis while teachers of older students may prepare fewer lessons that can be taught more than once a day.

Middle school teaching is notorious for the amount of work involved. In addition to all the necessary planning, middle school teachers have heaps of grading and note taking to do. On top of this, they often have homerooms filled with students who then become the teacher's responsibility. Homeroom teachers must remain abreast of their students' performance and progress to help them succeed. Much of this requires teachers to help students keep organized and reminded of school events. Homeroom teachers at the middle school level communicate with parents as well, not only concerning their sons and daughters but also concerning news and policies of their school's administration.

As this book explores in the next chapter, people who wish to teach at the middle school level will have to enter training programs that certify teachers in adolescent education. Like high school teachers, middle school teachers must choose a single subject area in which to be certified, be it math, English, art, and so on.

HIGH SCHOOL TEACHING

By high school, students should be taking on more responsibility for themselves, not only in terms of academics but in other more personal and social ways as well. High school teachers engage their students in a higher intellectual level of study, in some cases venturing into college-level material. Teachers at this level need to have a specialized understanding of their subject since high school courses are more concentrated in individual subjects. In many states, high school curricula and textbooks are designated by the state board of education. Therefore, many high school teachers are not allowed to create their own course of study but must implement standards set by the state in order to prepare their students for the required standardized tests.

Teaching at the high school level offers several other benefits. In some cases, high school teachers may have shorter workdays than teachers of other age groups. This opens up the possibility of becoming involved with a club at school or with some other vocational endeavor after school. Teachers who coach or run other clubs at the high school may be offered extra pay for additional time and commitment. Many high school teachers also benefit from periods of the day designated for lesson planning. Public high school classes can be larger than elementary or middle school classes, ranging from twenty-five to thirty-five students.

High school teachers assist in their students' preparation for college in a number of ways. Teachers aim to raise their students' skills and knowledge to a level at which they succeed when they enter college. Writing ability, organizational skills, and study habits are all explicitly reviewed and sharpened in high school, whereas at the college level these skills are expected. Teachers may also become college advisers in the sense that they can relate their own experience and knowledge about college programs. High school teachers are also asked to write recommendations for their students' college applications. In addition, teachers can put students in contact with people who are familiar with specific colleges of interest. These contacts can include alumni or students currently enrolled at the college.

COLLEGE TEACHING

College teaching remains an alluring goal for many teachers. Most classes do not start until later in the day, discipline is not an issue, and the intellectual content of course material is more challenging and engaging than that designed for younger people. However, establishing a career as a college professor remains difficult for several reasons.

First, fewer full-time positions are available at the college level than at lower levels of schooling, partially because many colleges hire adjunct faculty. An adjunct professor is someone employed part-time to teach single classes or complete other temporary assignments. In this fashion, colleges can avoid the expenses required to attract, pay, and provide insurance benefits to full-time faculty members. Adjunct professors are "let go" when they are not offered courses in future semesters. Since these part-time professors are paid minimally, have no guaranteed future at the school, and are not offered benefits such as a retirement package or insurance program, they find that making a living as an adjunct professor is nearly impossible. However, thousands of teachers accept these jobs because they can begin to build résumés that will one day help them secure full-time employment at colleges and universities.

At the minimum, college-level teaching requires a master's degree in the subject to be taught. However, a master's degree does not ensure a position. Colleges with job openings are flooded with applications from teachers who have strong college transcripts, lists of books they have written, real-world professional experience, and solid experience with teaching. Those wishing to pursue college teaching should start building strong professional profiles as soon as possible. Securing a teaching assistant job while in a master's program can be a great way to start. Many schools also enlist their graduate students as instructors for undergraduate-level classes.

Community college could be another starting point. Although positions at community colleges are also competitive, they are slightly less so than at four-year colleges. In general, teachers in non-academic fields—such as computer science, engineering, and business—have a smaller pool of applicants to compete against. As such, they have an increased chance of securing a position.

Full-time faculty members at institutions of higher learning enjoy a number of benefits. In addition to a good salary, subsidized health insurance, and a retirement package, college professors can also be offered time and resources for their own research. Tenure is another benefit. It is a way of protecting professors from political swings within their school administrations. After being reviewed and cleared by a special panel, eligible professors are granted tenure, meaning that virtually the only way the professor can lose his or her job is if he or she resigns. Therefore, tenured professors can never be fired, unless they commit some major offense. College faculty members on a tenure track at regular four-year universities usually need a Ph.D. in their field.

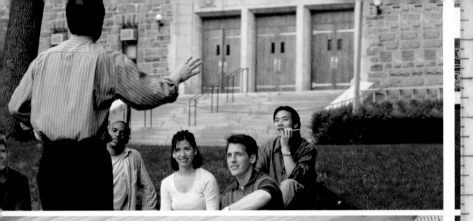

CHAPTER 5

DIFFERENT PLACES, DIFFERENT SCHOOLS

Schools can vary dramatically depending on their environment. A number of factors shape the way schools look on the outside and function on the inside. One way to think about different schools is to organize them into three groups: rural, suburban, and urban. This chapter offers some insight about how schools might vary depending on their surrounding communities.

RURAL SCHOOLS

Rural schools usually draw from a large geographic area. For example, rural high schools gather students from various smaller middle schools in the area. Therefore, rural schools do not necessarily have significantly smaller class sizes than urban or suburban schools.

Rural schools do differ in some ways, however, since the wider communities they draw from differ from urban and suburban populations. In general, rural populations exhibit lower household incomes and higher illiteracy rates. As a result, rural students sometimes have fewer role models that can support them in their education. However, rural communities are often very strong and tightly knit, priding themselves on family values and the absence of the violence characterized by city life. Rural schools represent communities in that same spirit, in the sense that many rural schools' faculties, administrations, and students form a kind of family of their own. Another perk in favor of teaching in a rural area is that public school salaries are the same as those found in urban areas, but the cost of living in rural surroundings is considerably lower than that in an urban environment.

Rural school districts sometimes struggle for resources. Property taxes provide less support because of the lower property values. Also, there is a tendency for rural property owners to approve budgets that underemphasize education. Funding from the government is not enough to provide the materials, technology, facilities, and teachers' salaries to attract the educators necessary for a complete and thorough education for rural students. In particular, schools have a need for technology. Compared to urban and suburban areas, rural homes and schools are disproportionately lacking in computers with Internet access. This scarcity combines with the absence of other cultural resources, such as museums, libraries, and concert halls, to affect young people's knowledge and understanding of the world. Although it is safe and family oriented, the rural community can be, in some respects, a very small one for both students and teachers alike.

SUBURBAN SCHOOLS

The nation's business executives and white-collar workers generally gravitate toward the fringes of urban areas in search of large properties and newly built housing. Families with high incomes and children often prefer suburban school systems that benefit from a high level of support

State	Total schools	Large city	Midsize city	Urban fringe of a large city	Urban fringe of a midsize city	Large town	Small town	Rural, outside MSA	Rural, inside MSA	Not applicable
Locale code										
United States	94,112	11,599	11,559	22,378	8,076	1,203	10,662	18,023	10,612	0
Alabama	1,526	95	259	131	212	10	294	291	234	0
Alaska	522	0	99	0	0	31	110	282	0	0
Arizona	1,815	707	164	421	30	33	160	189	111	0
Arkansas	1,153	0	248	8	98	11	281	402	105	0
California	8,916	1,658	1,153	3,988	626	42	253	523	673	0
Colorado	1,667	256	201	508	42	0	157	339	164	0
Connecticut	1,246	0	287	286	317	10	36	43	267	0
Delaware	199	0	40	76	23	0	20	26	14	0
District of Columbia	198	197	0	0	0	0	0	0	1	0
Florida	3,419	354	623	766	882	0	183	201	410	0
Georgia	1,969	98	208	535	96	33	336	341	322	0
Hawaii	279	75	0	94	0	0	0	97	13	0
Idaho	688	0	105	0	47	46	175	273	42	0
Illinois	4,351	604	476	1,476	183	63	499	654	396	0
Indiana	1,980	190	321	322	131	55	262	370	329	0
Iowa	1,521	0	243	1	126	65	360	623	103	0
Kansas	1,431	90	166	167	11	51	266	568	112	0
Kentucky	1,459	72	124	210	75	46	294	543	95	0
Louisiana	1,540	217	216	228	186	15	202	295	181	0
Maine	711	0	51	12	64	0	125	392	67	0
Maryland	1,385	181	49	804	12	0	37	101	201	0
Massachusetts	1,908	145	415	830	116	1	30	86	285	0
Michigan	3,984	315	519	1,075	467	0	400	560	648	0
Minnesota	2,408	307	112	776	82	25	369	533	204	0
Mississippi	1,037	0	120	22	99	51	322	350	73	0
Missouri	2,380	282	155	525	75	30	364	688	261	0
Montana	871	0	50	0	25	15	123	632	26	0
Nebraska	1,307	125	68	57	10	21	215	739	72	0
Nevada	531	102	52	167	38	12	37	94	29	0
New Hampshire	472	0	54	76	0	14	110	138	80	0
New Jersey	2,430	87	189	1,822	0	0	0	0	332	0
New Mexico	793	111	64	62	33	89	169	233	32	0
New York	4,351	1,318	265	1,184	489	15	291	268	521	0
North Carolina	2,234	112	493	81	265	24	329	519	411	0
North Dakota	569	0	66	0	23	19	72	343	46	0
Ohio	3,912	482	409	1,001	468	59	344	604	545	0
Oklahoma	1,824	236	91	291	14	50	319	654	169	0
Oregon	1,300	137	134	285	46	33	224	254	187	0
Pennsylvania	3,251	399	218	808	495	9	330	323	669	0
Rhode Island	333	0	116	0	163	0	6	7	41	0
South Carolina	1,145	0	174	19	325	0	166	247	214	0
South Dakota	762	0	68	0	14	0	104	539	37	0
Tennessee	1,646	290	198	147	172	25	254	356	204	0
Texas	7,761	1,862	1,116	1,673	414	82	872	999	743	0
Utah	791	0	139	0	341	28	102	157	24	0
Vermont	392	0	13	0	27	0	85	238	29	0
Virginia	2,090	150	353	460	256	16	152	436	267	0
Washington	2,233	130	377	703	140	27	207	349	300	0
West Virginia	822	0	82	30	121	12	144	368	65	0
Wisconsin	2,212	215	357	251	188	24	350	579	248	0
Wyoming	388	0	59	0	9	11	122	177	10	0

This table by the NCES provides detailed information on the distribution of public elementary and secondary schools by community type and by state. Reviewing information such as this can tell you where the students and schools are and, in turn, where the jobs are.

from a variety of sources. The financial resources available in suburban areas are translated to an enhanced educational experience for students of all ages. A large portion of those voting on budgets are parents who want to make sure their schools have all the tools they need to properly educate their children. In addition, suburban school systems feature bureaucracies that are smaller and more efficient than their urban counterparts.

Technology is recognized as a key aspect of succeeding in the global marketplace, so many suburban schools have a high computer to student ratio to help with research, creative projects, computer proficiency, and access to library catalogs.

Parents in suburban areas can support schools through direct involvement in clubs for languages, sports, and the arts. Evidence of this can be seen in the massive crowds at football games and the professional quality of school productions of plays and musicals. Suburban schools feature the best of rural and urban worlds: strong communities and family values paired with access to the cultural resources of the nearby cities.

URBAN SCHOOLS

Urban public schools, like rural schools, remain in crisis. Numerous indicators support this statement, among them statistics on student achievement, dropout rates, attendance patterns, and the retention of teachers. Urban communities find it difficult to properly support their schools, something that is compounded by urban boards of education, which are often large and inefficient bureaucracies. So, what money is available does not make it into the classroom. When making requests or asking questions, teachers dealing with many city board of education offices face long lines and computerized phone-in systems.

Despite these problems, urban schools still attract students, parents, and teachers for a number of reasons.

For example, some cities have developed a system that allows students to apply to any public high school within city limits in the same fashion that older students apply to college. Motivated students and parents can choose from a variety of schools according to their interests, geographic locations, and academic levels. Teachers who work in urban public schools insist that cities hold some of the most inspired teachers and students. Graduates of urban public schools win a large percentage of science and math awards each year. Cities also contain some of the finest cultural resources available in the nation: opera houses, jazz clubs, dance halls, planetariums, professional sports teams, and a variety of museums.

REGIONAL DIFFERENCES IN SCHOOLS

As you consider your options and preferences, you may wish to consider how schools vary regionally across the nation. As a teacher, your credentials and experience will transfer, with some red tape, to any state or area that attracts you. However, don't think that public schools are the same wherever you go. Always do some traveling in areas you are considering and interview people who have some relationship with schools—teachers, students, or other role players. Don't just move south because you think the weather will be milder. Depending on who you are, the social climate may not be as agreeable to you. Those moving east may be surprised at how people interact at work and in public, particularly in northeastern cities such as New York or Boston. In fact, America is large enough to be composed of a number of distinct cultures, each with their own customs and language. Schools are not exempt from these cultural differences.

In particular, states can have specific and contrasting philosophies that end up affecting the education that occurs in their classrooms. The political nature of states can be deeply reflected in education in a number of ways. Generally speaking, some states are conservative and some are more liberal or progressive. Examples of this might include Oklahoma, with its openly stated discomfort with evolutionism, or Vermont, with its groundbreaking support of programs in special education. In some cases, textbooks are approved or rejected by politically biased parties. This means that textbooks are not chosen by individual teachers but by bureaucrats in departments of education. Textbook companies cater to the political figures making the decisions—such book publishers add, omit, or amend information to please officials in these offices.

You may wish to look up a state or city department of education to review its mission statement. Also, you may search for news articles about special programs and initiatives that individual states are implementing. Some states are desperate for teachers of all types, while some states are searching for teachers of specific subjects such as math or science. States view licensed teachers as valuable resources and use a variety of means to attract them. In particular, programs that aim to fill vacancies in the most needy urban and rural areas have proliferated since the mid-1990s. Ask around to find out just what different states are doing and which may be offering incentives that are attractive to you.

Domestic Vs. International Opportunities

Much talk of globalization exists around the world, and the language increasingly used by various populations is English. Some call this phenomenon a process of Americanization in which U.S. values and preferences for dress, entertainment, and food are mimicked. Therefore, teachers are sought who are fluent in English and have an understanding of American beliefs and customs. Although most opportunities for teaching in foreign countries are offered by small, extracurricular, private programs that serve students of all ages, numerous foreign schools operate just like private schools in the United States. These schools are often independent day schools that attract a mix of children of American parents living abroad and native-born students. These schools help students of all ages participate in an American-style curriculum while simultaneously learning the host country's language and culture.

Although teaching positions at American and other international schools in foreign countries are quite competitive, these schools do hire teachers on a permanent basis using criteria similar to private schools within the United States. Most schools require teaching experience and a college degree in the subject being taught. Because the rewards of living in a foreign environment are enticing and the salaries are competitive, teachers in international schools tend to stay with their positions for long periods of time. School schedules and vacations match those commonly set in American schools.

Do an Internet search of international schools to find school listings, links to school Web sites, and job opportunities. Teaching in a foreign country can be both exciting and practical. Skills that are acquired while teaching abroad—including proficiency with a foreign language, experience with non-American populations, and skills teaching English as a foreign language—are useful for securing teaching jobs in the United States, too.

CHAPTER 6

CHOOSING A CONTENT AREA

I f you are going to teach above the elementary school level, you will have another choice to make—what subject you want to teach. The five main subjects in middle and high schools are English, math, science, social studies, and history. But numerous other subjects continue to be part of students' lives. This section offers you some insight into what it is like to teach different subjects, including the unique responsibilities, skills, and characteristics that teachers associate with each subject. You may just find yourself leaning toward a particular area because of the thought processes, skills, and materials involved with teaching that subject, even if your grades in that area have not been strong.

SOCIAL STUDIES AND HISTORY

History can be taught as a long story, filled with distinctive characters, events, and high drama. Teachers find that there is a certain creativity involved in bringing these stories to life and, more important, to helping students research and relate to world events, both past and present. Numerous subjects are included within the realm of social studies, including U.S. history, global history, civics, religion, philosophy, economics, psychology, sociology, geography, and government. Therefore, teachers who receive their certification in social studies must shift between these subjects on any given day. So, those of you who are interested in history or other social studies should prepare yourself to teach a number of different subjects over the course of a school year. You should realize that your training will need to be broad rather than specialized in any one area.

Today's students often take for granted the historical struggles required to ensure their liberty and their freedom of speech, voting, and so on. Young people may be interested in learning about their own cultural heritage as well as the changing nature of racial and gender relations. Many students grapple with fear and confusion stemming from recent clashes between terrorist groups and national governments. As a teacher of history, you will be able to shed light on the nature of these and other world conflicts as you give students the sense that they can play an active role in shaping the future.

MATH

Many students of all ages dread math and question its significance in their lives. However, math teachers understand that the study of arithmetic, geometry, trigonometry, algebra, and calculus involve thought processes that will prepare students to attack and work through problems in all spheres of life. Math requires clear, logical thinking and the ability to record the thought process in a concise manner. Math teachers need to find ways to make abstract problems interesting and real for their students. They also need to prepare students for math sections on state and other standardized tests. Because public school math teachers are often required to teach a set curriculum geared toward these tests, it is the responsibility of these teachers to offer the best materials and guidance they can to help students succeed.

SCIENCE

Science explores the nature of the universe, the earth, and life itself. The education of science continues to evolve with respect to new discoveries but has continued with its aim to train students to prove universal truths using a process called the scientific method. In other words, science teachers challenge their students to look at the world around them in a scientific light and to recognize the laws of nature that are in effect all around us. Because of the considerable differences within the field of science, ranging from biology to chemistry to earth science to physics, science teachers must choose a single area of specialization. Each area has its own methods, tools, and objectives, so science teachers are required to become certified in their area of specialization. For instance, if you want to be a biology teacher, you must earn a degree and certification in biology. Even though significant differences exist among the science disciplines, all science teachers must have training in safety and first aid because of the danger presented by the equipment and substances used in science laboratories. In particular, biology teachers must be trained in CPR (cardiopulmonary resuscitation).

ENGLISH

English teachers have great flexibility in what they teach and how they conduct their classes. For example, they often have lists of novels from which to choose. Using such texts as a starting point, they can create any number of class and homework exercises. English teachers focus on effective reading and writing skills but may venture into areas such as creative writing, debate, essay writing, speech, and autobiographical diaries. These skills are regarded as essential to success in any sphere of life. English teachers often have a very large workload, mostly consisting of stacks of papers to read and grade. While reading papers, English teachers must not only correct grammar, spelling, and punctuation but also keep a sense of each student's understanding of the issues he or she is discussing.

ART

Across the nation, budgets for art programs are constantly being slashed. Some school districts have even resorted to sharing teachers who travel between schools, even on a daily basis. Public school art teachers, like academic teachers, are given guidelines and standards set by states. Art teachers may also be required to train their students in a predetermined set of skills. This helps increase their students' success rates with awards, acceptance into college-level art programs, and special art reviews that allow students to test out of required courses once they are in college. Just like academic teachers, art teachers have to grade student work and establish criteria for doing so. Art teachers typically describe their daily lives as physically active, since they are constantly moving around their classrooms setting up projects, helping students, and cleaning up between classes. Another responsibility for art teachers may be the need to order, receive, and keep track of expensive art materials for the projects they plan for their students.

PHYSICAL EDUCATION

Even though most physical education (PE) departments seem separate from other departments within their school, PE teachers resemble academic teachers in a number of ways. These teachers usually work long hours and must plan lessons, give grades, manage groups of students, and have a solid knowledge base in their area of specialization. PE teachers must instruct students in the basics of sports and fitness, and also infuse the values of sportsmanship and teamwork into their classes. Their jobs may be regarded as even more challenging because of the large groups of students they instruct, their after-school duties, and the possibility for a sudden change in plans due to weather conditions. Yet PE teachers are fortunate because students do not feel the pressures often associated with academic classes; therefore, they tend to relax more during PE classes. Generally, PE teachers are not in high demand at public schools where the more fundamental academic programs are emphasized. Additionally, PE teachers must go through intensive training programs to become qualified. Most of the jobs in physical education are found in private schools that can afford to have more extensive programs.

TEACHING ENGLISH TO SPEAKERS OF OTHER LANGUAGES (TESOL)

English as a Second Language (ESL), English as a Foreign Language (EFL), and Teaching English to Speakers of Other Languages (TESOL) all involve teaching English to people whose first language is not English. EFL involves traveling overseas to teach English to people who are still living in their homelands, while ESL educates students living in English-speaking countries who have grown up using a different language. The goal of ESL often involves helping students with language barriers break into mainstream programs. It has the advantage of allowing one to work within the context of an English-speaking culture. Such teachers can greatly benefit from knowledge of their students' native cultures and languages, especially for teaching lower-level class students who need some guidance in their own language. Simply being a native English speaker does not qualify you to travel the world as a teacher. However, teachers who go through TESOL, EFL, or ESL training certainly have a world of opportunities open to them. TESOL, EFL, and ESL teachers are in demand at all levels of schooling, including colleges and universities.

COMPUTER SKILLS

In 2004, nearly 100 percent of U.S. schools, public or private, had at least some form of Internet access. In 2001, the average public school contained 124 instructional computers. These facts indicate that schools have a need for teachers and students with computer skills as well as faculty who know how to set up systems, keep them running, and train others in their use. Computer skills are of growing use in today's society, and schools are a place where those at a socioeconomic disadvantage can gain exposure to computers. Computer classes are increasingly offered at schools of all levels. These classes familiarize students with the basics of computer use, from keyboarding to producing documents with a variety of software programs. Computer skills instructors may work directly with teachers in other subjects to give students the chance to improve and give more color and depth to their academic class projects.

VOCATIONAL SCHOOLS

Most people think of vocational schools as programs that follow the completion of high school. In general, this is correct. However, vocational programs are starting to proliferate for high school students who are not interested in traditional academic coursework and have come to realize that they need to begin preparing for a practical career. These specialized high schools often aim to produce workers who are in demand by area employers, in fields such as health care, business, automotive repair, communications, and technology. School programs that partner with local companies and factories are also able to tailor their curricula to offer extremely relevant training for their students.

Teachers in vocational schools, both at the high school and post-secondary level, generally teach using an industrial or laboratory setting in which students receive hands-on training. Even though students are training for jobs that do not require a college degree, they do receive some instruction in regular academic subjects as a way to help them with their future occupation and home management. An example of this would be "practical math," which helps students exercise skills that they will need both on and off the job. Vocational teachers are similar to regular college faculty in that they must prepare lessons and grade papers along with all the other responsibilities of being a teacher. However, for students at vocational schools, the emphasis rests not so much on continuing with education but rather on moving directly into a real-world job situation. Vocational schools also facilitate this transition from college or high school to work by organizing internships and making information on prospective employers available to their students.

OTHER SUBJECTS

Of course, a variety of other subjects are taught at schools that call for teachers with experience and specialization. Think about what is offered at your own school. Those of you at private schools may have religion classes. Those of you at larger schools may have performing or theater arts classes offered. Health is a required part of the public school curriculum. Too many subjects exist to list here, but do not be discouraged if your passion is Latin or music. Whatever your interest, there are schools offering programs to qualify you to teach these subjects. Schools need teachers of a wide variety of subjects.

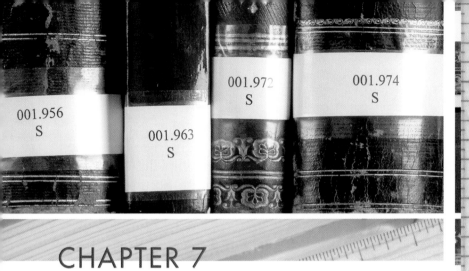

001.956
S

001.963
S

001.972
S

001.974
S

CHAPTER 7

DIFFERENT THEORIES IN EDUCATION

At one time, education was intended for only the wealthiest. As late as the end of the nineteenth century, schools taught classical languages, a small selection of great books, the history of the Western world, and other academic fundamentals. The teacher was regarded as the source of knowledge and authority, while students were meant to be obedient and considered to be ignorant. However, the twentieth century witnessed an upheaval in the field of education. Conventional forms of education were challenged for various reasons, including whom they educated, what they taught, and how they taught. Various alternative philosophies of education were born and have established new missions for schools, new goals for students, and new ideas for what teacher-student relationships should be. Some of these alternative types of educational programs are listed in this chapter.

PROGRESSIVE EDUCATION

In the early twentieth century, philosopher and educator John Dewey launched a school of thought that was labeled as a "liberal" or "progressive" way of thinking about education. Dewey and his colleagues in the Northeast sought to instill democratic values such as justice, equality, and creativity using projects that were derived from students' interests. These projects would incorporate important concepts from all academic subject areas. A classic example would be the construction of a kite, which requires understanding of aesthetic, scientific, mathematical, and logical principles. This brand of education contrasts with more conservative or "classical" classroom situations in which teachers stand at the front of the room and students sit quietly and absorb information. A number of states have adopted progressive education and implemented it as the central philosophy for their public schools. Examples of this can be found in senior projects that are designed by the students themselves and require the use of skills in a variety of subject areas.

Montessori schools embody these ideals as well, taking as a motto, "children teach themselves." Montessori schools are usually private elementary schools. The founder of this movement, Italian educator Maria Montessori (1870–1952), believed that students direct their own education naturally through real experience, even when unassisted by adults. Montessori schools use hands-on exercises and attempt to create a lively, colorful, positive learning environment.

QUAKER FRIENDS SCHOOLS

Originating from devout Protestant communities in the eighteenth century, Friends schools aim to provide an education that recognizes and nurtures the spirit in each child in relation to a community of learners. Today, Friends schools attract students from a wide range of religious, ethnic, and socioeconomic backgrounds. Such schools are marked by their emphasis on individual participation in a larger community, which is illustrated by their special method of holding group meetings. Even the youngest children participate in these meetings that systematically offer each member of the group a chance to speak without interruption. Parents turn to Friends schools because these schools give social skills and values as much emphasis as regular academic skills. Quaker teachers prevent conflicts between students through training in discussion and problem-solving techniques.

COMMUNITY-BASED EDUCATION

Increasingly, community service hours are required for graduation from middle and high school programs. In their most basic form, such schools make suggestions and organize events where students can do work outside of school on a volunteer basis. For example, students help out by cleaning up graffiti, visiting senior citizens, or tutoring young children. Some schools have adopted community service as a central aspect of their mission. These facilities assert that community-based education helps students apply the lessons they learn in the classroom to real-life situations and experiences.

In the field of science, students may participate in efforts to record and prevent the destruction of certain natural environments. Young artists may help beautify features such as fire hydrants, benches, or walls surrounding community gardens. In this fashion, learning can take place in businesses, community organizations, political offices, parks, and museums. Community service projects increase a student's awareness, interaction, and engagement with the communities outside of school. Vocational programs also take advantage of this model to provide students with experiences that simulate real-life work situations.

Giants in the History of Education

Confucius (500 BC, China) Confucius was famous for human examples and aphoristic sayings, which became well-known proverbs. Some of these include "The desire to learn is most important," "Self improvement by friendly rivalry between fellow students," and "Good teachers are good students." Confucius's philosophy was fundamental to the culture of China and several populous eastern Asian countries. His philosophy would become the basis for education.

Plato (428 BC, Greece) Plato devised a method through which a teacher could help arrive at the truth with a student's assistance: the dialogue. Plato also helped develop the method of hypothesis, the recollection theory, and a theory in which all ideas, virtues, and objects have ideal and perfect counterparts in a higher realm.

John Dewey (1859–1952, United States) Dewey philosophized on the nature of education, as in his book *Democracy and Education: An Introduction to the Philosophy of Education* (1916). He presented a progressive philosophy in which education was directed by and centered around the student.

Maria Montessori (1870–1952, Italy) Montessori is credited with the development of the open classroom, individualized learning, "manipulative" learning materials (that is, teaching toys), "learning by doing," and programmed instruction. Today, Montessori schools are still guided by the philosophies of their namesake.

Mary McLeod Bethune (1875–1955, United States) Adviser to president Franklin Roosevelt and founder of the National Council of Negro Women, Bethune is known as a social reformer and educator. The focus of Bethune's career was the betterment of young African American people. The centerpiece of her career was Bethune-Cookman College in Florida.

Jean Piaget (1896–1980, Switzerland) Piaget believed that children are primary agents in their own education and development. Human behavior, he stated, was an adaptation of the person to the environment.

James Baldwin (1924–1987, United States) Baldwin was a widely known African American essayist, novelist, and playwright. Born and raised in the Harlem ghettos of New York City, he became one of the most eloquent voices in the struggle for civil rights in the United States, which, among many other social changes, championed equal education regardless of race.

Organizers of these projects insist that such interactive exercises enhance the social and economic health of the involved communities.

SPECIALIZED HIGH SCHOOLS

Across the country, but particularly in urban public school systems, an increasing number of high schools offer specialized courses for students with special talents and interests. Such schools may emphasize science, mathematics, engineering, or the arts, or they may offer advanced courses in all subjects. Public schools with these profiles often require that entrance exams and in-depth applications be submitted to fill a limited number of spaces. Schools that offer special opportunities in the visual arts often require portfolios, while schools specializing in the performing arts—such as theater, dance, and music—base their admissions decisions on auditions held for eighth- and ninth-grade students.

Specialty high schools compete with private schools in terms of the quality of the education and the performance of their students on tests, college acceptance, and award competitions. The school's curriculum offers more in-depth and advanced opportunities for study and training than regular programs can afford. Students are often more driven and committed to their interests, and they are required to take more credits in certain areas to receive a diploma from one of these specialized schools.

EXPLORING THE VARIETY OF TEACHING SITUATIONS

The diversity of U.S. students creates a need for a wide variety of teachers. Specialization within this field continues and calls for increasing numbers of teachers with expertise and experience. As you develop yourself as a teacher, your career may take unexpected turns and could lead in a number of different directions—different types of schools, different age levels, or different specialties. You may even find yourself moving in and out of the field of education. Remember, experience gained along one career path will be invaluable even for job opportunities that seem to have little in common with the particular type of teaching you have tried. Feel free to explore without the fear that you are closing off opportunities as you make choices to teach in certain situations. Teaching can be a fantastic way to grow and find out more about the world and about yourself. Teaching takes you different places and puts you in contact with different people. You will only discover what type of teaching suits you by trying out opportunities in various schools, in different regions within the United States, and even possibly in foreign countries.

As you enter into positions at schools—as a volunteer, an assistant, or a full-time head teacher—you will want to increase your awareness of each situation and how it contrasts with positions at other schools. This will help you succeed and gain the most beneficial experience from the time you spend in any particular situation. Individual schools can be seen as cultures with their own distinct characteristics—places that have developed their own kind of languages and customs. As you gradually understand a school's culture, you will become a contributor and important part of that culture. Even if you feel that your own personality, philosophy, or teaching style conflicts with the situation you find yourself in, you will still be learning and affecting the traditions of that school. Schools have certain identities but also require diverse voices within them to keep them healthy and in a constant state of growth. As an individual in a school, you will always represent your own background, culture, and family. As you engage yourself in a school, you will undoubtedly be contributing to and enriching the lives of the people around you in a variety of ways. In fact, you may be shaping the way future generations perceive your type of school, subject area, and teachers in general.

CHAPTER 8

GOING TO SCHOOL TO BECOME A TEACHER

As you might have guessed, quite a bit of training and schooling awaits you on your way to becoming a teacher. In some ways, you will always be learning and educating yourself in ways that will help you teach others. As a matter of fact, as a teacher you should, and may be required to, continue attending classes to keep up with new information, technology, and techniques all the way up through retirement!

This chapter focuses on the degrees and certifications you will need to earn on your path toward accepting your first teaching job. Everyone is different, so keep your own situation in mind as you read through the descriptions of these educational options. Some people are pressed for time, others want to try teaching before they fully commit to it, some know now that they want to earn the highest level degree from one of the most prestigious universities, and others know the exact age level or subject area they want to work in. This chapter aims to describe the various paths teachers take as they begin and continue to build their careers. It should be useful to you regardless of your own particular goals and dreams as a teacher.

At the very least, you will need a college-level (or postsecondary) degree for nearly any secure full- or part-time teaching position. Your degree need not be directly related to education, but if you don't pursue education as an undergraduate, earning a degree in one of the main academic subject areas (math, science, history, or English) will increase your chances of being offered teaching jobs in the future.

You cannot do too much research as you explore and weigh the pros and cons of postsecondary programs. This is an extremely difficult process because it requires you to ask yourself some challenging questions about who you are and where you want to direct yourself. The choice of a college program relates to the creation of your own identity. This process involves professional and personal aspects, both of which must be considered in order to make the most of your experience. Because you are a unique person, the best way to research programs is to ask people who have experience with the programs you have targeted. In your discussions, be sure to explain yourself and your goals as clearly as you can. Don't be embarrassed by a lack of knowledge or understanding—education can be a complicated field that is in a continual state of change. By clearly stating what you believe any given college program will provide for you, the people with whom you speak will have a clearer understanding of how to guide and advise you.

College catalogs try to sell you on their programs just as an advertisement attempts to convince you to make a purchase. College programs may be one thing on paper but another thing in reality. Many factors are involved—such as school reputation and changing faculty members—so you need to keep abreast of what is happening (and what people perceive is happening) at any given school. Entering into a college-level program requires a huge investment of time, energy, and money. Once expended, none of these can be easily recovered. Making the proper choices today can save you a great deal of frustration. All college-level education programs offer some balance of focused training and general education. Just as college programs try to balance this mix, so should you. Keep yourself focused on specific goals while being mindful of how your schooling and experience may be applied to a number of different career paths.

In any case, education after high school can be a lot of fun. Some teachers get into education because of the experiences they enjoyed as students, not to mention the teachers that inspired them. Use your postsecondary school experience as a place where you can observe and learn from your teachers as teachers, not just as masters of the subjects they teach.

CHOOSING A TYPE OF COLLEGE PROGRAM

This section will take you through a number of types of college programs, from the most basic to the most advanced. All can lead to positions in teaching, but you should keep in mind that for public school teaching, you will, at least in the long run, have to make your way through a master's level program. There are a variety of approaches to doing so, each of which differs in terms of time required, the nature of the education, and the cost. Costs and details about paying for college follow in the next chapter. This section will help you familiarize yourself with the college programs that are available for you as you progress toward that first teaching job.

JUNIOR COLLEGE

Junior colleges, community colleges, and other two-year, college-level programs can be a viable option for those who are interested in becoming teachers. Junior colleges allow two types of approaches to teaching. In the first, the student uses the junior college program as a springboard to a larger four-year program. Since classes are less expensive and may require slightly less intense work, students use these programs to warm up to a more intensive college program. Most credits earned at two-year programs can be applied to full bachelor's degrees.

In the second option, students complete a two-year program that qualifies them for positions as assistants. Assistant teachers are sometimes referred to as paraprofessionals. Junior colleges, which offer focused training for specific professional occupations, award associate's degrees. Although an associate's degree may be a short-term goal for you, considering the number of cheap, quick, and easy degrees being offered online, you should realize that this type of degree will not take you very far in the world of education. But it can act as a solid first step on a longer journey. As you look at junior college programs, you will notice mention of their "accreditation." Accreditation is a method of certifying schools to ensure that they meet national or state standards. Accreditation is monitored by independent agencies assigned by the U.S. Department of Education. Take note of who has accredited the program and exactly what the program will qualify you to do.

LIBERAL ARTS AND SCIENCES DEGREES

Liberal arts and sciences colleges and universities offer a broad familiarization with courses ranging from the sciences to the humanities. (Humanities include literature, philosophy, languages, and cultural investigations.) Students generally enter these four-year programs directly or soon after graduating from high school, although students of all ages participate as well. The NCES estimates that 1.33 million bachelor's degrees will be awarded in 2005, with a greater number of women than men earning degrees. More and more students become "double majors" because of a strong interest in two academic areas. A double major requires more courses to be paid for and completed, but it shows a greater commitment and a wider scope of knowledge. In general, the liberal arts curriculum requires a set "core curriculum." This includes the basics of both sciences and humanities that must be completed in order to graduate.

Education can be pursued as a major at the undergraduate level. Some colleges offer either bachelor of arts (BA) or bachelor of science (BS) degrees in education. These programs lay out a sequence of courses that require study in both general liberal arts and a wide range of professional education courses. Students in four-year college programs have the opportunity to explore a wide variety of subjects as well as the chance to focus and engage in more in-depth study in the field of education. In fact, many states require that education majors take on at least one other content area like math or English as a part of their study. In addition to regular coursework, educational programs at four-year colleges organize and require a certain number of hours of fieldwork and student teaching in school or related environments. Nearer to the end of the program, students are required to become student teachers—they teach their own classes under supervision for a certain number of hours. Four-year liberal arts programs allow students to investigate educational theory, gain experience through practice, and test the latest in educational technology. Students who are aware of their desire to teach in the early years of their adulthood will undoubtedly be rewarded by the in-depth study offered by a four-year program.

One important aspect to realize about college programs, and not just liberal arts programs, is that certain majors and specialties within these majors may or may not be available at any given institution. Also important is that not every college has education as a major! But don't fret. Any liberal arts education presents a solid foundation from which to begin nearly any career. As mentioned earlier, you should consider majoring in one of the primary content areas because the credits you earn in these traditional academic areas will help you earn higher degrees, qualify for jobs, and get into master's education programs later on. But even if you don't end up graduating with a degree in math, English, science, or history, you will still be building strong skills in research, writing, and problem solving, not to mention a broad base of knowledge in Western and other civilizations. For those with the time, money, drive, and intellectual curiosity, four years of college presents an important opportunity to build a strong academic foundation that will support you in various ways.

For those who graduate from four-year college programs without any coursework in education, there are two possible paths that lead to teaching. The first route leads to teaching at private schools, which require only a BA degree for entry-level positions. For those seeking jobs in public schools, the second path requires additional schooling. The most obvious choice would be a master's program that condenses all of the coursework, fieldwork, and student teaching into an intensive program aimed at getting you into the classroom quickly. Graduating from college also qualifies you to participate in special programs that allow teachers to work and earn money while simultaneously earning master's degrees and certification. These programs are described in the next chapter under the heading "Alternative Programs for Untrained Teachers." In either scenario, earning a four-year degree, even if the degree is earned in a major other than education, offers not only a strong academic foundation but also a number of options within the field of education.

BA/MA PROGRAMS

Some larger universities offer a few opportunities for combining a BA and an MA degree. This takes just a little more time than it requires to earn a BA by itself. In general, students interested in these opportunities would initially apply for entrance into the university as a regular, full-time undergraduate student. Then, after the successful completion of about two years of course credits, they would apply for a BA/MA program. Once a student is admitted into this type of program, he or she must complete the courses, fieldwork, and student teaching required for a full master's degree while finishing off the credits required for the undergraduate degree. Since there may be some overlap between these two curricula, students in BA/MA programs may be required to take fewer classes than those who complete the two programs separately. Oftentimes, courses are offered at both the graduate and undergraduate level, covering the same material but at a greater depth and with more assigned reading and writing at the graduate level. Usually, BA/MA programs require that the courses applied to the master's degree be taken at the graduate level, but not always.

MASTER'S IN EDUCATION PROGRAMS

Sometimes abbreviated as MAT for master of arts in teaching, these programs follow the completion of bachelor's degrees. In most states, teachers aiming for full-time employment at public schools will eventually need a master's degree, even if the teacher is originally hired before he or she has received this degree. Master's degrees are the most common and traditional method of attaining the qualifications for teaching. Master's programs generally take about one full year, summer included, of full-time study. Since many of the students in these programs are working, schools allow part-time study and make required courses available in the evenings after work. On a part-time basis, it may take up to three years to complete all the necessary credits, fieldwork, and student teaching projects. Many of the students in this category are already teachers who are able to use their paid teaching experience to satisfy field-work and student teaching requirements, as long as they are teaching the subject and age level in which they aim to earn their degree.

Full-fledged master's programs offer a wide range of specializations. When applying, students must indicate a single area of focus, choosing between special and regular education, early childhood (grades kindergarten through sixth), and adolescent education (grades seventh through twelfth). For those entering adolescent programs, applicants must choose a content area in which to specialize. For teachers of adolescents, master's programs can take longer to complete if the teacher entering the program has not majored in the content area he or she has chosen. Upon acceptance, these students may be informed of some additional coursework in that content area that they must complete to be allowed to graduate.

When you check out the variety of offerings available within master's in education programs, notice how some specializations qualify you to teach a wider range of students by age. For example, degrees in music or dance enable you to teach students from pre-kindergarten to twelfth grade.

As different levels and types of education increase, so does the level of specialization. You may be surprised to see how degrees qualify teachers only within small segments of the field of education. Teachers are being asked to make more focused decisions as they shape their careers. For example, those going to school in special education must usually pick one of a number of specializations within that broad category, be it education for the deaf, behavioral disabilities, learning disabilities, severe disabilities, and so on.

At completion of your program, you will receive one of a number of different degrees. Some schools offer master of sciences in education (MS.Ed.) degrees, some grant master of arts (MA) degrees, and some master of education (Ed.M.) degrees, depending on the school and the specialty you have chosen. So, for example, a student on his or her way to teaching math at the high school level would strive to earn an MA in teaching with a specialty in adolescent mathematics (quite a mouthful!). In addition to granting these degrees, master's programs help their students obtain certification in their area of specialty. (Details on certification follow in the next chapter.) Master's programs also facilitate job placement by offering career advising, résumé building services, job conferences, and connections with schools. Master's programs have experienced professionals available to help you navigate the bureaucracy and red tape as you prepare to start as a full-fledged teacher.

DOCTOR OF EDUCATION PROGRAMS

In some sense, master's programs help students establish a base for research skills in education. Teachers with significant experience, a master's degree, and the drive to continue with an advanced education may consider a doctor of education (D.Ed.) or a doctor of philosophy (Ph.D.) in education. Doctoral programs are extremely selective, require years of commitment, demand a substantial amount of master's level coursework, and culminate in a final thesis project of the doctoral candidate's choosing. Doctoral theses range from pure scientific research to formal studies of sociological, cultural, and historical aspects of education. As coursework for these advanced degrees is completed, students may also earn master of arts or philosophy (MA or M.Phil.) degrees along the way. Once completed, doctors of education become qualified to teach education courses at the college level and are considered more seriously for tenure than those without Ph.D.s. Many teachers in elementary and secondary schools finish their careers without completing a Ph.D. program.

Moving into a Program of Study

For Americans, the choice of a college program can be one of the most important decisions of a lifetime. The decision you make will impact your professional and personal life. This choice can be overwhelming because of the seemingly infinite number of options. Choosing a college requires that you not only research as many programs as possible but that you understand yourself in terms of your own goals and abilities. Various constraints affect nearly all people wishing to find a fitting college program, including factors such as the cost of these programs, their distance from your home, and the range of opportunities they offer, among others. You may feel that you don't have the time or resources to conduct proper research for such a huge decision. This section will show you how to take advantage of the events and tools you can easily access to help you make an effective choice.

Choosing a College

Traditionally, printed college catalogs are a primary resource for young people researching college programs. School libraries or college advisement offices usually collect these colorful folders containing pictures, descriptions of program and degree offerings, historical and current information about the college, and an application. If you can't find a suitable copy of a catalog for a college you may want to attend, you can contact the college directly and have one sent to your home address. However, college catalogs are being posted on the Internet more frequently. On the Web, you will find a wealth of information at your fingertips. You may also wish to refer to listings of colleges that are organized like large phone books. These listings pare down each program to its most basic information, including academic opportunities, special programs, regulations governing student conduct, social environments, sports opportunities, costs, and student demographic information. *The Princeton Review*, *Fiske*, *U.S. News and World Report*, and many other publications print these directories. Some are geared to certain types of people, such as minorities or those seeking inexpensive programs. There are even listings of college programs that serve those with learning disabilities. Remember, if you can't find any of these resources, you may request that your college adviser or librarian order them for your entire school community to use.

You may also be able to take advantage of meetings with college representatives at your school. If you're overwhelmed by the prospect of organizing a trip to visit colleges that interest you, check to see if those colleges are sending representatives to your city, town, county, or school. If your top choices are not scheduled to make visits, try the following: First, submit a list of schools to your college adviser and ask about the possibility of having such colleges send representatives to your school. Second, go ahead and sit in on meetings with representatives from colleges that you may not think you are interested in attending. Just listening to a presentation on a random college program can really help you focus in on things that are important to you.

APPLYING TO COLLEGE

You may think it's best to apply to as many colleges as possible, but the application fees can add up quickly into hundreds of dollars, so you should pick a short list of colleges that vary in characteristics and competitiveness. Another reason to minimize your applications involves the amount of materials they require: personal essays, recommendations from teachers, and recommendations from others who know the applicant. Application forms can be

As competition to be admitted to college programs increases, applying to undergraduate and graduate programs has also become increasingly more complicated. Many programs ask for several letters of reference, as well as a personal statement of interest.

difficult to do well, especially if you try to do too many. For those of you who are more certain about your desire to become a teacher, make sure you emphasize this goal in your essay. Also, be sure to describe your plans when you ask teachers to write recommendations for you. The admissions panel that reviews applications needs to pull out some concrete facts about you and who you are becoming. Be as clear as possible with your intentions, but also mention a willingness to explore new ways of thinking. Although many programs do not require a personal interview with a college recruiter, this can be an excellent opportunity to express and distinguish yourself from the thousands of others applying for the same program. If you are able to travel to a college campus, be sure to take advantage of guided tours and the chance to meet current students. Don't be shy! Colleges foster environments where people can ask casual questions and strike up light conversations.

What Do College Programs in Education Entail?

Let's take a closer look at what education programs include. This section provides a general sense of what education majors are required to do to fulfill their requirements and attain their degrees, whether it be undergraduate or graduate-level degrees. To some extent, states have some control over the requirements established in college programs—for instance, the number of hours of required student teaching. This occurs because the state ultimately grants certification in any given specialization within teaching. States also approve or disapprove college programs, so make sure that any program of interest is, in fact, registered with the state, leads to state certification, and is accredited (that is, supported) by state education offices. Colleges and government agencies unite in the overall goal of producing educational courses that are designed to develop competent classroom teachers.

In general, education programs detail a sequence of courses in which hands-on skills can be attained in parallel with an exploration of relevant fields of knowledge. More specifically, programs outline a course of study that includes student teaching, academic classwork, and some form of focused final project. Therefore, students striving for degrees in education will be spending some time in the classroom as a student but will also have many hours in other classrooms either observing or conducting their own classes as student-teachers.

CURRICULUM CONTENT

Students are required to pass a variety of academic courses in a broad range of subject areas. Education degrees include study of the philosophy of education, which requires students to analyze, critique, and further respond to different ways of pedagogy. ("Pedagogy" is a fancy word for what is taught and how it is taught in schools.) Some credits must also be earned in child psychology, particularly the psychology of the age group you're planning to teach. Another major aspect of the academic course load involves what is sometimes called "methods," or the way a specific subject or age group could and should be taught. Methods courses explore means of assessing student progress through tests, essays, portfolios, and so on, as well as approaches to classroom management, dealing with parents, unit and lesson planning, and the incorporation of state standards into the curriculum. In addition to these core classes, college-level education programs usually require a small number of credits of basic computing skills, health, and safety. Some of these classes, such as presentations on dealing with child abuse, drug use, and violence prevention, may meet only once or a few times. Also, for teachers of adolescents (at the middle- and high-school levels), students will have to complete coursework in their chosen subject area—for example in math, English, or music. Master's programs in adolescent education will demand that in addition to the standard curriculum, the prospective teacher takes some courses in the subject area if he or she has not completed the basic requirements at the undergraduate level. Some master's programs may not even allow the teacher to be accepted until these required credits are completed.

STUDENT TEACHING

Student teaching is a required element of teacher certification programs. Teachers-in-training must instruct for a certain number of hours in the subject and age level in which they wish to be certified. Student teaching assignments may be coordinated independently, but college programs offer assistance in locating and making these arrangements as well. Some college programs even have their own elementary, middle, and high school programs that are directly affiliated with the college. These schools may be located near the college campus or at a remote location. In any case, students seeking certification must design curricula, plan lessons, grade papers, keep records, and log notes in conjunction with a faculty member from the college program. Together, the professor and the teacher work through the challenges associated with what are, in some cases, the teacher's initial attempts at actual teaching. For others, it is not their first attempt because they are already employed in schools when it comes time to take on a student-teaching assignment. If they are teaching the same subject and age level of the certification they are seeking, they may use their paid work as the basis for their student-teaching projects. However, if they are teaching a different subject or age level during the day, they must make arrangements to teach at either another school or with another set of students at the same school.

Take a look at the teacher training programs that interest you to determine the number of hours of student teaching you will be required to complete. Usually, student teaching appears in listings of course requirements alongside the other courses. That is, you will be earning a certain number of college credits and receiving a grade for your student-teaching project. This student-teaching course usually lasts one entire semester, with about sixty days of actual student teaching.

CAREER PLACEMENT

Although this is not part of your required coursework, you should take advantage of the career placement services offered through your college program. Most colleges have a career-placement office with at least one full-time staff member who is available to assist you in a variety of ways. At the career placement office, you will find listings of job openings, notices of internships, addresses of schools, and information on other placement services. By scheduling an appointment with career-placement professionals, you will be able to build and edit your résumé, discuss options, and practice your interviewing skills. You may be able to establish a file at the placement office that can be opened for school administrators seeking teachers. Career-placement services will also coordinate events that will put you into direct contact with those responsible for hiring teachers. Sometimes, these events take the form of conferences featuring representatives from school districts or placement agencies. After these school "reps" are given a chance to speak about what they are looking for in prospective teachers, they may be available for a short meeting and to exchange contact information. Although this can be an effective way of gaining exposure to schools seeking teachers, some career-placement offices require fees for various services.

JOB FAIRS

College programs will keep you abreast of job fairs held around the country throughout the year. By attending a job fair, a candidate can meet with administrators from several schools in a short period of time—even schools from a wide range of geographic areas. These fairs recruit for either private or public schools, but rarely both simultaneously. For teachers interested in private schools, another chance to learn more is at the annual conference hosted by the National Association of Independent Schools (NAIS). Such conferences are filled with so many speakers, presentations, and workshops that it is impossible to experience them all. You will have to choose to attend those that appeal to you most.

Job fairs for public schools occur frequently across the nation. They are usually sponsored by a small group representing different boards of education seeking to attract teachers. A quick search online using the keywords "public school job fairs" will return plenty of links describing these fairs.

CHAPTER 9

CERTIFICATION

All of the teacher training programs described in the previous chapter assist teachers in gaining their credentials. Teacher credentials come in many forms, go by different names, and differ from state to state. While it would be impossible to describe in detail every state's system for formally accepting teachers, this chapter offers an introduction to the various types of credentials required for today's teachers.

"Certification" is a variation of the word "certificate," which describes a formal document that is granted by an institution or agency. Certification is a key step toward becoming a schoolteacher. Although it is not required for teachers aiming to start in private schools, certification shows a level of commitment and training that may provide an edge when interviewing for private school positions as well. However, a teacher must be certified by a state government agency in order to be hired as a teacher in a public school in that state. So, whether you have completed a graduate program in education or you have entered an alternative program that allows you to teach while studying, certification will

State	Basic skills exam	Subject matter exam	General knowledge exam	Knowledge of teaching exam	Assessment of teaching performance
1	6	7	8	9	10
Alabama	(\1\)	(\2\)		(\2\)	X
Alaska	X				
Arizona		X		X	X
Arkansas	X	X		X	X
California	X	(\3\)			
Colorado		X		X	
Connecticut	X	X			
Delaware	X				
District of Columbia	X	X			X
Florida	X	X	X	X	X
Georgia	X	X			
Hawaii	X	X		X	
Idaho					
Illinois	X	X			
Indiana	X		X	X	
Iowa					
Kansas				X	
Kentucky	(\1\)				X
Louisiana	X	X	X	X	X
Maine	X		X	X	
Maryland	X	X		X	X
Massachusetts		(\4\)			
Michigan	X	X	(\5\)		
Minnesota	X		X	X	
Mississippi		X		X	
Missouri	(\1\)	X		(\6\)	
Montana	X				
Nebraska	X				
Nevada	X	X		X	
New Hampshire	X	X			
New Jersey		X	(\7\)		X
New Mexico	X		X	X	
New York			X	X	
North Carolina	(\1\)	X			
North Dakota	(\1\)		X	X	
Ohio\8\		X		X	X
Oklahoma	X	X	X	(\9\)	X
Oregon	X	X			(\10\)
Pennsylvania	X	X	X	X	
Rhode Island\11\			X		
South Carolina	X	X		X	X
South Dakota\12\	X	X			X
Tennessee	(\13\)	X		X	X
Texas\14\		X			
Utah				(\15\)	
Vermont	X				
Virginia	X	X			
Washington	(\1\)				
West Virginia\11\	X	X		X	X
Wisconsin	X				
Wyoming	X				

This chart, provided by the NCES in 2002, demonstrates the assessment for certification by state. The numbers indicate slight variations to the requirements, which you can learn more about at each state's department of education Web site.

be your short-term goal. Certification is often confused with licensure, since in some states the two terms are interchangeable. For instance, some states require licensure but not certification. However, in some areas, certification would be attained first, before a specific license is granted. Think of it this way: if you want to drive a car, you will need a license. If you decide to go through driver's education, you will receive a certificate saying that you passed. Once you have this certification, you are able to go and apply for the license. The process is similar for teaching, but it gets confusing because states are often involved in both the certification and the licensing. This confusion deserves a little bit of attention. The following sections explain certification and what you have to do to become certified. Further details on licensure are provided after that.

Certification is handled differently in various states, but two basic types of certification generally exist. Although most boards of education prefer to hire certified teachers, in some states the great demand for teachers has necessitated the employment of individuals who have not been trained and certified. Therefore, some educators are allowed to teach using temporary certifications— called provisional or conditional certification—depending on the state. States grant certificates that declare the teacher's specialization by subject area and age group. For example, in any given state, certificates for teaching academic subjects for grades seven through twelve may include English, mathematics, social studies, and so on. Certificates for regular elementary school teachers do not specify a subject area.

A teacher may also hold more than one certification. Some teachers take advantage of opportunities in BA/MA programs or master's programs in which they take on extra coursework and testing on a path toward receiving dual certification. In some cases, the number of extra courses required for dual certification may be minimal, especially through the use of College-Level Examination Program (CLEP) exams. By taking these tests, teachers can prove their abilities in order to receive credit for college-level courses or place automatically into advanced courses more directly. Although these tests require a fee and some preparation, they can save time and money en route to earning either a single or dual certification.

PROVISIONAL CERTIFICATION

In most cases, an individual who has met all the requirements established by the state would first seek a temporary certificate, usually referred to as a provisional certificate. For example, a prospective teacher can apply for certification only upon completion of all academic coursework, student teaching, state-mandated workshops (such as those on child-abuse identification and school-violence prevention), applicable standardized tests, fingerprinting, and a security review. The provisional certificate is an entry-level certificate that is issued for a specific subject and grade. It is valid for a limited period of time, usually about five years. The teacher must complete the requirements for a permanent certificate before the provisional certificate expires.

In general, teachers may apply for provisional certification only upon graduation from an accredited teacher-education program. For example, those in the final semester of a graduate program would apply for their provisional certification through the program office, where forms and applications are made available. Staff at the graduate school assists in the application process by reviewing applications, double-checking that qualifications are met, guiding students through the process of fingerprinting, and ensuring that applications are properly processed. The application may require a seal from a notary public or a fee in the form of a postal money order. After the graduation ceremony, an official copy of your college transcript completes the application. All materials are then forwarded to the state office.

You may expect some sort of written confirmation that the paperwork has been received, as well as an estimate of how long it will take to approve the application—between one and three months.

Essentially, a provisional certification is required to enter and teach in public schools. States with programs that recruit teachers without a degree in education offer a special provisional certification, even before many important requirements have been met. However, these programs do require you to enroll and begin coursework en route to a master's degree in education. In this type of situation, you will have a time limit for fulfilling all of your coursework, student teaching, testing, and so on. Later in this chapter, in the section on alternative programs, you will find more information concerning this approach to becoming a fully certified teacher.

PERMANENT CERTIFICATION

Although provisional certification is a short-term goal for teachers, it is just one step toward permanent certification. The process of certification differs depending on the state, yet permanent certification may require a provisional certificate, two years of teaching in a public or nonpublic school, a completed master's degree, and a passing score on applicable certification tests. An individual who holds more than one provisional certificate may meet the two-year experience requirement with any two years of paid full-time classroom-teaching experience. For instance, a teacher who holds the pre-kindergarten through sixth and English seventh through twelfth certificates could satisfy the experience requirement for both certificates by teaching for two years in an elementary classroom or two years as a secondary English teacher, or a combination of such experience totaling two years. In some states, a video demonstrating a few of the teacher's classes may also be required. Once all of these requirements have been completed, the teacher must pay a fee and apply for the certification. The application, like the application for the provisional certificate, must include verification of completion of a master's program and other required training programs.

INTERNSHIP CERTIFICATES

At participating colleges and universities, students may qualify for a graduate internship program after completing around 50 percent of their degree requirements. These certificates allow the teacher to begin teaching in public schools. The teacher must be nominated and must complete an application and interview process. Internship certificates are valid for only a short period of time (for example, two years) and remain valid only if the teacher remains in good standing both as a teacher in his or her school and as a student in the teacher-education program.

TRANSFERRING CERTIFICATES TO ANOTHER STATE

Some states will issue certificates to teachers certified in other states. There must be an interstate agreement between the states, so you may want to review the list of states you will have access to with the certification you receive in your own state. Sometimes these certificates are called conditional provisional certificates or transitional teaching certificates. Once this type of certificate is received, teachers must pass all of the teacher certification exams required by the target state within a set amount of time, usually within two years.

LICENSURE

As mentioned earlier, the word "license" with regard to teacher qualifications can mean different things in various states. In some states, there is no certification, only licensing. In many other states, however, a pedagogical license is a temporary permit (often referred to as a credential) that allows the educator to teach a certain subject to a specific age group for a limited amount of time. This contrasts with certification because once you are certified, it can never be taken away under normal circumstances. Although certification is granted by state agencies as a means toward controlling the content of teacher-training programs, licenses may be granted not only by states but also by departments of education, such as those in major cities. After the teacher earns his or her certification, there is yet another application, interview, and screening process that must be completed before the teacher receives the license. Licensing agencies may or may not honor certifications earned in other states. In some areas, a teacher would apply for a license only after being offered a specific job. Teachers can only receive a license for the specific area and age levels in which he or she is certified. Indeed, an individual may apply for a license in every area for which he or she has a valid state certification. However, in some states, a teacher may be appointed and serve under only one license at a time. In most cases, once a teacher is appointed under a license, he or she begins a three-year probation period. Licenses may, in fact, be revoked if the teacher neglects his or her duties, commits a crime, or engages in some other inappropriate activity.

The pedagogical license application requires a number of documents. First, a copy of the permanent, provisional, or conditional certificate must be attached. If the application is based on certification from a different state, you may be asked to include proof that you have initiated the certification process for the state where you want to teach. Likewise, if you applied for a certificate within the same state but have yet to receive it, you may need to submit proof that you completed your teacher-education program. Proof of completion of special workshops on child abuse and other subjects may also be required, along with test scores for required teacher certification tests. All relevant college transcripts, including those from your teacher-education program, will have to be attached as well. Finally, a lengthy application that includes your contact information, educational background, work experience, and teaching experience will need to be submitted. References are also required. For those of you with no prior work experience, you will need to list at least two personal references. Such references are from people who have known you for an extended period of time and can describe the quality of your character. Since licenses are issued by public agencies, you will have to affirm that you have not been convicted of a crime more severe than a misdemeanor, that you have never had a pedagogical license revoked or suspended, and that you have never been dishonorably discharged from military service. Security measures also require that teachers be fingerprinted if they have not already been required to do so in the certification process.

The licensing system helps state and local boards of education keep track of their teachers. Because licenses must be renewed to continue teaching, educators may be required to complete additional training programs and security checks periodically to keep records up to date with changes in research and state policies. This system further strives to ensure the quality and character of the teachers in the nation's classrooms. It offers governing authorities the power to revoke licenses and thereby keep irresponsible teachers out of classrooms.

ALTERNATIVE PROGRAMS FOR UNTRAINED TEACHERS

A number of programs have been designed to attract teachers to areas of high demand. These programs often target individuals with no prior experience or training in teaching. Although the salary and benefit packages offered can be very attractive, the conditions for teachers participating in these programs can be quite challenging. Some programs, like the nationwide Teach for America, are designed for young adults (eighteen and older) who have just graduated with a bachelor's degree. Others are more localized, such as the Teaching Fellows Program in New York City, which attracts individuals of all ages, including those looking for a change of career. These alternative programs differ in the level of support they offer teachers as such educators work through graduate school toward permanent certification. Some will pay full tuition at certain colleges and universities (usually public institutions), while others simply offer a dollar amount that can be applied toward teacher-education programs. Others take care of student loan payments during the term of service. Such alternative programs offer teachers an opportunity to gain experience, earn a salary, receive benefits, complete requirements for master's degrees, and attain certification simultaneously.

Although some alternative programs offer substantial advantages, in reality they can be extremely challenging. First of all, teachers entering these programs may have little say in the location of their placement or of the school where they are assigned. With nationwide programs, you may not know exactly where your teaching assignment will take you, although you will have the opportunity to state your preferences in terms of region, type of school, and age level. If the program is locally based, you will know the city or county in which you will be working, but you will not be able to control your choice of school or class. These programs are created to attract teachers to the most difficult situations, usually in poor rural and urban communities. Most likely, teachers in these programs will be placed in situations with little support from the school administration, scant resources and materials with which to operate, and students who have severe learning and behavioral issues. The application process for these programs usually requires a face-to-face interview as well as written work. The screening committees realize the nature of the work and will select teachers they feel are up to the challenge. Although salaries and benefits are attractive, you should be careful as you consider these programs. Don't be discouraged if, after applying, you are not accepted initially. Alternative programs are meant for certain types of people who are flexible and strong enough to deal with unfamiliar and difficult situations.

YOUR EVER-CONTINUING EDUCATION

You should realize that your education as a teacher is something that began the moment you entered your first school and will continue through to your retirement. Even after you receive advanced degrees, whether you must study due to strict licensing requirements or conduct your own continuing education independently, you will always be building on past experiences and adapting to new developments in the field of education. Even if you are a seasoned teacher, taking classes can remind you of the joys, frustrations, and issues involved in being a student. Keeping this in mind will increase your effectiveness as you, in turn, strive to teach others.

Indeed, your career in education can lead you in multiple directions. Since career mobility is a feature of American society, anything you achieve for your career in teaching can help you move in other directions as well. Your accomplishments—such as education degrees, acceptances into special programs, or awards—are worth their weight in gold with regard to careers inside and outside of the sphere of education. Everything you learn from nonteaching work experience, hobbies, your personal life, your family, and even travel will help your work as a teacher. The best teachers understand how to incorporate all aspects of their lives into their lessons. They know how to regard their students as important human beings who have strengths, weaknesses, and lives of their own. As you develop as a teacher, you should be able to observe and learn from all of your experiences to make your life a truly educational experience that can be passed on to your students.

CHAPTER 10

WEIGHING THE COSTS AND BENEFITS OF TEACHING

The number one misconception about teaching is the idea that teachers are not well paid. When compared with other careers, teaching appears to be something done not for the money but out of a humanitarian concern. Certainly, teachers are not compensated as well as lawyers, doctors, and professional athletes, but they are able to afford a good standard of living with benefits that will last into retirement.

One of the most significant aspects of the practicality of teaching involves the great demand for teachers. Although a demand for teachers exists in certain areas and specific types of schools, the general demand for teachers is strong and continues to grow. Therefore, teaching offers the opportunity to obtain and secure a job, not to mention long-term financial independence. Particularly at the beginning of the new millennium, the demand for trained and experienced teachers of all types has driven up salaries, sweetened benefits packages, and opened up a wide variety of opportunities for teachers around the world. In light of the vacations, afternoons, and evenings that may be used for other pursuits, teaching becomes a terrific option. Time spent training, earning credentials, and gaining experience with teaching is certainly time very well spent. Teaching is indeed a practical career choice.

This chapter presents a cost-benefit analysis from which you may draw your own conclusions. A cost-benefit analysis is a classic economic exercise that takes into account all of the costs associated with a certain enterprise and compares them to the benefits of a similar endeavor. A difficult aspect of cost-benefit analysis is the many intangible elements involved. For example, the fact that most teachers enjoy their jobs, the personal rewards gained from teaching young people, and frequent paid vacations are hard to factor into an analysis that measures benefits in terms of dollars. This chapter will not be able to present all of these elusive factors, but it will explore the more concrete costs and benefits of teaching.

COSTS ASSOCIATED WITH TRAINING TO BECOME A TEACHER

You will have to invest in yourself if you wish to become a teacher. Investment involves sacrificing money, time, and energy for a payoff that will come later. The most obvious cost associated with preparing to be a teacher involves the fee of the required degrees you will have to earn along the way. On occasion, education in America has been described as an industry that aims to market itself in order to attract customers and make money. As with any other product that is for sale, teacher-education programs can vary greatly in terms of cost and quality. Just as cheap coffee will not taste as good as some premium roast, you can try to save money with teacher-education programs, but the quality of the programs available at lower prices may suffer in comparison to the quality of education in the more expensive programs. The price of education programs is most often determined by the dollar amount paid per credit, or credit hour. Most college courses are offered on a semester basis and are three-credit classes. A three-credit class would generally meet for about three hours per week, either two ninety-minute sessions per week or one three-hour class.

BA/MA programs allow teachers to complete requirements for two degrees in a relatively short amount of time and with less cost. By completing the BA and the MA separately, you are required to take an additional twenty credits. Since a full-time student would generally take about fifteen credits in any given semester, a BA/MA program allows students to earn two degrees with only one semester of extra work. Many teachers have to work and study at the same time. Therefore, for those teachers who are teaching while completing college credits on a part-time basis, twenty credits could represent two full years of study and thousands of extra dollars. Therefore, if you have yet to decide on a course of study and you are committed to a career in education, BA/MA programs represent the most time- and cost-effective way of becoming a fully qualified teacher.

The required credits at individual schools may vary slightly, and credit hours may also be affected by courses that you have or have not already taken. Also, credits you earn in one program may be transferred to other programs in the future. Some instances may occur where you would have to complete additional credits in order to satisfy all the requirements for your degree. For example, a student who wants to become a math teacher but did not major in

Credit Requirements of Degree Programs

Let's take a look at some of the numbers concerning degrees one can earn on his or her way to becoming a teacher. The following table shows the number of credits required for each type of degree:

Associate's Degree (65 credits): Associate's degrees can be attained in a short amount of time but do not qualify you for many jobs. They can be a good way to transition from high school into a four-year college program.

Bachelor of Arts/Sciences Degree (120 credits): Also known as under-graduate degrees, these degrees usually require about four years of full-time study. College students seeking BA/BS degrees must choose a major.

BA/MA Programs (140 credits): BA/MA programs combine the course-work of both the undergraduate and the graduate degree into a shorter, cost-effective program. You must apply for these programs after the first year of undergraduate work. These programs are intensive, requiring a great deal of coursework in your chosen field.

Master's Degree (40 credits): Master's degrees are required for public school teachers. When applying to these programs, teachers must choose an area of specialization such as high school history or special education.

You should use the preceding figures as a general guideline as you consider your options for your own course of study.

mathematics as an undergraduate would be required to take additional courses to make up for missing credits.

THE VARYING COST OF COLLEGE CREDITS

Colleges determine tuition costs in one of two ways. First, they charge a flat rate for full-time students, meaning that full-time students pay a single amount for an entire semester's classes. In the second, examined here, colleges charge according to each individual credit. Of course, from college to college, the cost per credit will differ greatly. In particular, private colleges and universities cost substantially more than public institutions. According to the NCES, average undergraduate tuition and room and board for the 2001–2002 school year were estimated to be $8,046 at public colleges and $22,520 at private colleges. This is a significant difference!

Furthermore, even within the same college, students may be charged differently. A number of factors contribute to the amount charged to any given student. For instance, in public universities, individuals who can prove that they have lived within the state for a certain amount of time would qualify for lower tuition rates as in-state residents. Those from out of state would then be non-resident students. This difference in tuition fees can be substantial as well. Also, students who enroll on a full-time basis are charged less than those who study part-time.

Tuition costs also differ for graduate classes and undergraduate classes. In general, students are charged the undergraduate rate until they have completed the number of credits required for an undergraduate degree. After that, the student has to pay the higher tuition all graduate students face. If this information seems overwhelming to you, don't worry! College catalogs and Web sites will explain clearly their policies on tuition. Be sure to compare the tuition costs of all college-level programs that interest you.

ADDITIONAL COSTS OF COLLEGE-LEVEL PROGRAMS

Tuition is just the beginning of the costs associated with going to college. First, if you are studying full-time, it will be difficult to work full-time. Some young teachers don't have the resources or support to get by on part-time wages, so many must resort to a full-time position immediately after high school. Full-time employment could be seen as a loss, also known as an "opportunity cost." But there are more obvious costs involved with college as well. For example, school supplies and textbook prices continue to rise dramatically. Also, you will have to feed, clothe, and house yourself during your years in college. For prospective teachers there are also costs for standardized examinations, vaccinations, doctor's examinations, applications, and fingerprinting. You should get an idea of these costs and make sure to include them as you develop your budget.

USING FINANCIAL AID TO REDUCE YOUR BURDEN

The costs of higher education can be substantial, but many resources are available to lessen the financial burden. Financial aid is available to both graduate and undergraduate students, coming in the form of scholarships, grants, loans, and work-study opportunities. Teachers in training initially look to the financial aid programs that have been established by the federal government, including Pell grants, Stafford loans, Perkins loans, and federal work study. Pell grants, which are gifts of money that do not have to be repaid, are available for undergraduates only. Stafford loans are low-interest student loans that must be repaid and are available to both undergraduates and graduates. If you qualify for a subsidized Stafford loan, the government pays the interest on the loan while you are in school. In 2004, first-year undergraduates are eligible for Stafford loans up to $2,625, with increasing amounts made available as students progress into graduate school. Perkins loans are likewise low-interest loans that must be repaid. In 2004, the maximum annual loan was $4,000 for undergraduates and $6,000 for graduate students.

Additionally, federal work-study opportunities may be available for students as a means of earning a decent wage that must be applied toward the cost of tuition or room and board. Work-study jobs usually take place somewhere on the college campus itself. Under all federal student aid programs, the student and his or her family are expected to contribute as much as they can afford to cover the costs of tuition, health insurance, and living expenses. A form called the Free Application for Federal Student Aid (FAFSA) includes the family's income information. By comparing the cost of the education with the family's financial situation, the expected family contribution is determined as the dollar amount for which the family and the student are responsible.

Federally supported education grants and loans can alleviate your financial burden, but you must check with each individual college program to make sure that the college offers the financial aid you need. Some schools do not participate in all of these federal programs, and some offer none at all! For students seeking to enroll in programs that do not offer federal assistance, or those who require more assistance than the government can offer through these programs, there are independent banks and lending agents that offer loans to cover the costs for tuition and living expenses as well.

Of course, after graduation, teachers will have to pay back their loans plus any interest that accrues in the meantime. Although some student loans do not charge interest until after graduation, some do. The interest rates can be very high. You may want to postpone payment for your education, but later on you will have to pay significantly more than you originally borrowed. Just like any credit situation, it is usually better to avoid borrowing because of the cost it incurs later on. In any case, as you consider the costs and benefits of a career in teaching, be sure to account for monthly loan payments when you plan your budget.

TEACHER SALARIES

Now that you have an idea of some of the costs of educating yourself to be a teacher, you're ready to move on to the good part: your salary. Individuals of all ages and backgrounds turn to teaching each year as a source of financial stability and independence. In fact, teacher's salaries have increased considerably over the years and are expected to keep increasing (even with respect to inflation) through 2025. As reported by the American Federation of Teachers (AFT), a national teacher's union, the average teacher's salary for the 2000–2001 school year was $43,250, while the average beginning teacher's salary was $28,986, up 4.4 percent from 1999–2000.

Teachers included in the survey had an average 15.8 years of experience, which indicates that although beginning salaries are substantial and rising on a yearly basis, increases after the first year are not as impressive. Even though teachers' unions decry this state of affairs, the fact that teachers' salaries are lower than salaries in other professions—such as computer engineering, sales, science, and law—should not be taken at face value because of the number of days a teacher works in the typical school year. In general, public schools are in session for around 180 days per year. Taking into account about a week of extra time for meetings and other preparation, teachers report to school only about 185 days in a year. Professionals in other areas work about 250 days of the year, having only weekends, a few holidays, and about ten vacation days. Accounting for this difference, the beginning teacher's salary of $28,986 would translate to a salary of $40,258 if the teacher worked a full 250 days. The average teacher earning $43,250 would earn $60,069 for a full year of work. Also note that teachers can take advantage of opportunities to increase their yearly income by working during vacations.

SALARIES BY REGION

The National Center for Education Statistics (NCES) periodically compiles reports on teacher salaries. These are updated periodically and available online. One of the reports compares average salaries by state, a figure that includes all public school teachers, regardless of the number of years of experience. For the 2001–2002 school year, New Jersey was reported as offering the highest average salary ($54,575), with Connecticut ($54,870), California ($53,870), and New York ($53,081) likewise offering high average salaries. These salaries compare with the national average in the 2001–2002 school year of $44,604. California has recently experienced a rapid rise in teacher salaries, increasing about 10 percent between the 2000–2001 and 2001–2002 school years. This reflects the state's efforts to reduce class size and attract additional teachers to do so. On a regional basis, Mid-Atlantic, East North Central, and Pacific states offer the most competitive salaries.

As reflected in the same NCES report for the 2001–2002 school year, the states with the lowest average salaries were South Dakota ($31,295), North Dakota ($31,709), Mississippi ($32,800), and Montana ($34,379). Other states substantially below the national average and below the $40,000 mark were Colorado, Georgia, Hawaii, Iowa, Kansas, Kentucky, Louisiana, Maine, Missouri, Nebraska, New Hampshire, New Mexico, Oklahoma, South Carolina, Tennessee, Texas, Utah, and Vermont. Referring to the table on page 111, you will find that on a regional basis, East South Central ($37,027), West North Central ($36,453), West South Central ($36,383), and Mountain ($37,790) states offered the lowest average salaries for the 2001–2002 school year.

For those of you looking for high salaries in your first year of public school teaching, the American Federation of Teachers has compiled a set of statistics that may interest you. For the 2000–2001 school year, the states with the highest average beginning salaries were Alaska ($36,293), California ($33,121), New York ($32,772), Delaware

Average Public School Teacher Salaries

Average public school teacher salaries by region and state for the years 2001–2002, as reported by the National Center for Education Statistics, *Digest of Education Statistics*, 2002

New England

Connecticut	$54,300
Massachusetts	$50,293
New Hampshire	$38,911
Vermont	$38,802
Maine	$37,100
Average	**$43,881**

Mid-Atlantic

New Jersey	$54,575
New York	$53,081
Pennsylvania	$50,599
Average	**$52,751**

South Atlantic

Delaware	$48,305
District of Columbia	$47,049
Maryland	$46,200
Georgia	$44,073
North Carolina	$42,959
Virginia	$41,262
South Carolina	$38,943
Florida	$38,719
West Virginia	$36,751
Average	**$42,702**

East North Central

Michigan	$52,037
Illinois	$50,000
Ohio	$44,492
Indiana	$44,195
Wisconsin	$43,114
Average	**$46,768**

East South Central

Alabama	$39,268
Tennessee	$38,554
Kentucky	$37,847
Mississippi	$32,800
Average	**$37,027**

West North Central

Minnesota	$43,330
Iowa	$38,230
Missouri	$37,695
Kansas	$36,673
Nebraska	$36,236
North Dakota	$31,709
South Dakota	$31,295
Average	**$36,453**

West South Central

Texas	$39,293
Louisiana	$35,437
Oklahoma	$35,412
Arkansas	$35,389
Average	**$36,383**

Mountain

Nevada	$41,524
Colorado	$40,222
Wyoming	$37,841
Idaho	$37,482
Utah	$37,414
Arizona	$36,966
New Mexico	$36,490
Montana	$34,379
Average	**$37,790**

Pacific

California	$53,870
Alaska	$49,418
Oregon	$43,886
Washington	$43,483
Hawaii	$41,951
Average	**$46,522**

($32,281), and Connecticut ($32,203). The states with the lowest average beginning salaries were North Dakota ($20,675), Idaho ($23,386), Mississippi ($23,292), South Dakota ($22,457), and Montana ($21,728).

Of course, the cost of living in these states and regions can vary considerably. Some reports account for the cost of living using a concept called purchasing power. A higher level of purchasing power would indicate that you can buy more per dollar in that area. For example, after adjusting for cost-of-living differences between states, the AFT reported the average teacher in Pennsylvania in the 2000–2001 school year had the highest purchasing power of $52,832, compared to an adjusted salary of $30,899 in Hawaii, where teachers have the lowest purchasing power. In this same study, after adjusting for a $9,419 drop in purchasing power, California's rank dropped from second to sixteenth out of the fifty states. Therefore, as you think about salaries available in certain areas, do some research on the cost of living in that area as well.

SALARIES FOR SPECIAL EDUCATORS

According to the U.S. Bureau of Labor Statistics, in 2000 the median salary for special education teachers was $40,880 at the preschool, kindergarten, and elementary level, $38,600 at the middle school level, and $41,290 at the high school level. The demand for teachers in special education is much higher than the demand for other teachers. Because of this, some local school districts offer stipends or signing bonuses to qualified special educators.

INCREASES IN SALARIES OVER TIME

According to the NCES, public school teacher salaries were projected to increase (taking inflation into account, that is, in "real dollars") each year between 2002 and 2003 and are predicted to increase in 2012 and 2013. Using a conservative estimate, teacher salaries are projected to increase to $47,400 in 2012 and 2013. This represents a 6 percent increase during this ten-year span. This estimated increase will follow a 4 percent increase from $43,100 in 1987 and 1988 to $44,900 in 2002 and 2003. On a similar note, the AFT reported that the average public school teacher salaries in 2000 and 2001 were 31.5 percent higher than they were in 1990 and 1991. Most forecasters predict that the salary increases of the past will continue, in real dollars, over the next several years.

ADDITIONAL FINANCIAL BENEFITS OF TEACHING

Salary is just one aspect of the financial support that a career in teaching offers. The benefits associated with teaching represent an added perk for those seeking long-term financial stability for themselves and their families. Generally speaking, these benefits include insurance, retirement packages, and vacations. Let's look into some of these areas in more detail.

HEALTH INSURANCE

Health insurance continues to be a controversial issue in American politics. In contrast with most other industrialized nations, individuals in the United States are responsible for their family's health insurance. Health insurance programs vary in quality and cost, but even the least expensive and most simple policies can cost hundreds of dollars each month. However, just like group travel plans, if you can gather more people together to buy at the same time, the cost per individual can be greatly reduced. Understanding this, employers often organize health insurance for their employees to reduce their expenses. Most private companies, private schools included, are able to provide this benefit for their employees only, that is, not their employees' family members. However, because public schools are state institutions, employees of schools can be grouped together into the same insurance program. The savings that result from this pooling of thousands of teachers are tremendous, allowing each individual employee's family (employee, spouse, and children) to enroll in the same program for a low fee. For teachers with families, particularly those with many children, this benefit becomes very important. Thousands of dollars can be saved over the course of a year.

RETIREMENT BENEFITS

Retirement benefits are another factor you should consider, even if you are just breaking into your twenties and thinking about beginning a career rather than ending one. Retirement programs gather money from salaries, invest it, and return the money with any profits to longtime employees after they stop working. These are sometimes called pension plans. Your goal for retirement should be to continue receiving checks on a monthly basis after you retire and stop working. This will allow you to continue with the lifestyle to which you have grown accustomed. As with insurance programs, companies can be more effective with retirement funds if they can pool groups of individuals together. By including more people in their programs, states can offer their public school teachers attractive retirement benefits. States set up retirement systems for all public employees, including teachers. These funds are particularly stable because they are backed by the government and supported by hundreds of thousands of participants.

The amount of retirement benefits you will eventually receive depends on the number of years you taught (in the same school system), the dollar amount contributed out of each paycheck, and your final salary (or some combination of your highest yearly salaries). Of course, the amount you contribute while teaching will most dramatically affect the amount you receive in return during retirement. Although there is a minimum amount that will be deducted from your paycheck, as a public or private school employee, you will be allowed to contribute larger amounts if you choose. The amount you contribute will be limited to some percentage of your salary. Whether you opt for the minimum or the maximum contribution, these amounts will be directly taken out of your monthly paycheck. In some cases, the money that you save in this fashion will be placed into an investment account with a mix of stocks, bonds, and mutual funds. The benefit of investing in this type of retirement plan rather than a regular investment account involves taxes. Any money you make on your retirement investments will not be taxed as long as you do not make any withdrawals before you retire.

Retirement benefits can be very complicated, and certainly vary from state to state. Private school teachers may not be allowed to start participating in retirement plans until they have worked at the same school for a certain number of years. Regardless of your particular situation, you should start planning now for retirement by including a monthly retirement savings payment in your projected budget. As with any type of investment, the more you save now translates into considerably more later.

OTHER BENEFITS

Independent private schools and public school systems try their best to provide as many benefits as possible to their employees. These come in a variety of forms, including assistance with transportation, various types of insurance, and help with certain purchases. For example, some life insurance is often a part of a teacher's benefit package in order to protect the teacher's family in the event of death. Another benefit many schools offer involves allowing some expenses to be paid using pretax dollars. In particular, transportation and medical costs, including prescription drugs, may be arranged to be paid automatically, before the teacher's taxable income is calculated. When the taxable income is lowered, the amount the teacher must pay to the government at tax time is reduced as well. Additionally, dental insurance will most likely be included in any teacher's benefit package. This insurance covers yearly checkups as well as some emergency dental procedures.

CHAPTER 11

AREAS OF DEMAND FOR TEACHERS

Attracting trained, experienced teachers is one of the most difficult tasks a school faces on a yearly basis. Because of increasing numbers of students, the schools' desire to expand their programs, and a decline in the number of individuals entering teacher preparation programs, this task becomes all the more difficult. In fact, teacher shortages remain acute in certain subject areas and locations. Schools sometimes have trouble attracting teachers that reflect the diversity of various student populations. Furthermore, school districts report a high rate of teacher attrition, which means the loss of staff members, and a need to replace experienced teachers who are retiring. Young teachers in particular are in a position to take advantage of this situation. By researching areas of high demand early, young teachers can take advantage of their interests and goals to create challenging, satisfying, and lucrative careers.

This chapter will help you learn about the areas in which new teachers are needed most.

OVERVIEW

According to estimates by the NCES, by 2013 student enrollment will rise by 4 percent in public schools and by 7 percent in private schools from their levels in 2002. Currently, the median age of teachers is forty-four years old, with more than 25 percent of all teachers reported as being fifty years old or older. Teacher attrition then becomes a major factor triggering an increased demand for teachers. To maintain the teachers needed to educate the estimated 56.4 million public and private school students in the year 2013, a great deal of hiring will occur in the first decade of the new millennium. The NCES estimates 150,000 to 200,000 job openings for teachers from 2002 to 2013. Trends toward decreased class size will further increase this demand.

Of course, America's schools are not just calling for teachers, but for qualified teachers. According to a 2002 report by the Education Trust, around one-fourth of high school teachers of main subject areas like English do not have college degrees in their subjects. By arming yourself with educational and vocational experience within a core subject area, you as a prospective teacher create opportunities for yourself in a variety of types of schools in various geographic locations.

DEMAND BY SUBJECT AREA

A 2002 report by the American Association for Employment in Education (AAEE) observed that no area within education is experiencing a surplus of teachers. Confirming a long-established trend, the most critical

Table 3: Educator Supply and Demand by Field and Region

Region codes: 1 - Northwest, 2 - West, 3 - Rocky Mountain, 4 - Great Plains/Midwest, 5 - South Central, 6 - Southeast, 7 - Great Lakes, 8 - Middle Atlantic, 9 - Northeast, 10 - Alaska and 11 - Hawaii.

Demand codes: 5.00 - 4.21 = Considerable shortage; 4.20 - 3.41 = Some Shortage; 3.40 - 2.61 = Balanced; 2.60 - 1.81 = Some Surplus; 1.80 - 1.00 = Considerable Surplus

Field	1	2	3	4	5	6	7	8	9	10	11	National 2000	National 1999	Change
Agriculture	—	3.40	3.50	3.64	3.00	3.08	4.11	3.25	3.67	—	—	3.43	3.50	-0.07
Art/Visual Education	2.78	2.59	3.56	3.11	2.83	2.97	2.91	2.65	2.56	3.00	3.00	2.90	2.78	0.12
Bilingual Education	4.80	4.54	4.63	4.33	4.68	4.42	4.18	3.62	4.33	4.00	—	4.38	4.32	0.06
Business Education	3.50	3.13	3.43	3.37	2.80	3.23	3.43	2.77	3.60	4.00	3.00	3.23	3.16	0.07
Computer Science Education	3.60	4.00	4.17	4.38	4.13	4.38	4.21	4.33	4.75	4.00	—	4.23	4.14	0.09
Dance Education	2.50	2.90	3.00	2.57	3.50	2.67	2.83	3.25	2.00	—	—	2.85	2.76	0.09
Driver Education/Traffic Safety	—	3.00	—	3.00	2.43	3.00	2.82	2.88	3.00	—	—	2.86	2.91	-0.05
Elementary Education														
Pre-K	2.50	3.70	3.38	3.25	3.15	3.43	3.11	2.82	3.00	—	3.00	3.17	2.88	0.29
Kindergarten	2.50	3.86	2.90	2.93	3.09	3.27	3.04	2.76	2.75	3.00	3.00	3.06	2.89	0.17
Primary	2.60	4.05	2.85	2.77	3.33	3.33	2.75	2.81	2.50	3.67	3.00	3.02	2.86	0.16
Intermediate	2.80	3.97	3.38	3.01	3.54	3.51	2.95	2.97	2.96	3.67	3.50	3.22	3.00	0.22
English/Language Arts	3.00	3.60	3.50	3.32	3.31	3.39	3.13	3.02	2.90	4.00	4.00	3.25	3.05	0.20
English as a Second Lang. (ESL)	4.00	4.16	4.67	4.36	4.60	4.05	3.96	3.89	4.63	—	3.00	4.19	3.98	0.21
Health Education	2.50	2.81	3.00	2.44	2.38	2.66	2.48	2.68	3.00	—	—	2.56	2.49	0.07
Home Economics/Consumer Sci.	—	2.88	3.67	3.94	3.50	3.35	3.80	3.22	4.67	—	—	3.52	3.57	-0.05
Journalism Education	3.00	2.80	3.00	3.08	3.08	2.83	2.88	2.83	3.50	4.00	—	2.99	2.90	0.09
Languages														
Classics	2.60	3.00	5.00	3.58	3.17	3.15	3.47	3.67	3.40	—	—	3.34	3.23	0.11
French	2.67	2.92	3.63	3.63	3.62	3.72	3.37	3.33	3.33	4.00	—	3.41	3.29	0.12
German	2.83	3.00	3.33	3.46	3.19	3.35	3.29	3.11	3.43	4.00	—	3.25	3.16	0.09
Japanese	3.38	3.36	5.00	3.33	3.25	3.20	3.83	3.71	3.50	4.00	—	3.52	3.32	0.20
Spanish	3.71	4.00	4.60	4.13	4.34	4.22	4.24	4.06	4.11	4.00	—	4.16	4.04	0.12
Mathematics Education	4.46	4.76	4.85	4.65	4.59	4.32	4.34	4.19	4.32	3.50	4.50	4.44	4.18	0.26
Music Education														
Instrumental	3.42	3.40	3.88	4.00	3.55	3.13	3.50	2.96	3.92	4.00	—	3.53	3.35	0.18
Vocal	3.33	3.16	3.88	3.93	3.50	3.04	3.50	2.96	3.75	—	—	3.47	3.31	0.16
General	3.00	3.39	4.11	3.81	3.17	2.98	3.32	3.24	3.50	—	3.00	3.37	NA	
Physical Education	2.50	2.70	2.82	2.45	2.59	2.66	2.57	2.76	2.67	3.00	3.00	2.60	2.54	0.06
Reading	3.50	3.83	3.43	3.43	3.52	3.42	3.47	3.46	3.27	4.00	3.00	3.48	3.43	0.05
Science Education														
Biology	3.62	4.39	3.90	4.11	4.10	4.21	3.83	3.95	3.96	4.00	4.00	4.04	3.88	0.16
Chemistry	3.92	4.66	3.90	4.42	4.35	4.31	4.39	4.38	4.37	4.00	4.00	4.36	4.17	0.19
Earth/Physical	3.55	4.48	3.80	4.15	4.03	4.20	3.98	4.00	4.00	4.00	—	4.08	3.90	0.18
Physics	3.77	4.58	4.11	4.40	4.26	4.37	4.50	4.51	4.40	4.00	—	4.40	4.26	0.14
General	3.38	4.17	4.11	4.05	3.96	4.07	3.77	3.71	3.81	4.00	5.00	3.91	3.86	0.05
Social Studies Education	2.67	2.59	3.15	2.71	3.00	3.11	2.47	2.56	2.67	3.50	2.00	2.73	2.45	0.28
Special Educaton														
Multicategorical	4.63	4.75	5.00	4.65	4.44	4.53	4.63	4.30	4.07	5.00	5.00	4.53	NA	
Emotional/Behavioral Disorders	4.50	4.50	5.00	4.65	4.50	4.52	4.73	4.60	4.20	5.00	—	4.59	4.39	0.20
Hearing Impaired	5.00	4.44	5.00	4.52	4.14	4.50	4.13	4.17	3.67	5.00	—	4.37	4.25	0.12
Learning Disability	4.56	4.68	5.00	4.56	4.50	4.54	4.38	4.32	3.82	5.00	—	4.46	4.36	0.10
Mental Retardation	5.00	4.64	5.00	4.47	4.38	4.45	4.36	4.31	4.00	5.00	—	4.44	4.33	0.11
Visually Impaired	3.50	4.67	5.00	4.50	4.00	4.20	4.58	4.33	3.33	5.00	—	4.38	4.18	0.20
Mild/Moderate Disabilities	4.38	4.67	5.00	4.65	4.57	4.55	4.08	4.35	3.89	5.00	5.00	4.45	NA	
Severe/Profound Disabilities	4.43	4.80	5.00	4.67	4.50	4.52	4.30	4.38	3.88	5.00	—	4.51	NA	
Early Childhood Special Ed.	4.29	4.23	5.00	4.46	3.64	4.31	4.21	4.05	3.13	5.00	—	4.20	NA	
Dual Certificate (Gen./Spec.)	4.00	4.54	4.80	4.33	3.82	4.32	4.06	4.36	3.91	5.00	4.00	4.23	NA	
Speech Education	3.20	3.78	3.00	3.28	3.17	3.50	3.09	3.85	3.33	5.00	—	3.33	2.84	0.49
Technology Education	3.80	3.93	4.00	4.44	3.40	4.31	4.20	4.54	4.29	4.00	3.00	4.17	4.03	0.14
Theatre/Drama Education	2.82	2.77	2.25	2.98	2.96	2.67	2.74	3.11	2.60	—	—	2.82	2.84	-0.02

Finding the right job in education may also depend on what's available. Be sure to watch different trends in teaching, such as teacher supply and demand by field and region. This chart, released by the American Association for Employment in Education (AAEE) in 2003, offers a good idea as to which fields need teachers.

shortages are reportedly occurring in the fields of physics, chemistry, mathematics, and computer science. The Recruitment of New Teachers, Inc. (RNT) is one resource for research on teacher demand. According to the RNT's 2000 study of the largest urban school districts in the United States, nearly 98 percent of responding districts noted an immediate demand for science teachers while 95 percent reported a present need for mathematics teachers. Because of the lack of qualified and trained instructors, mathematics and science positions are often filled by teachers without a major or certification in these fields. Areas of more moderate demand include the fields of foreign languages (particularly Spanish, French, and Japanese), vocal and instrumental music, agriculture, and home economics.

DEMAND FOR MINORITY TEACHERS

A major criticism of U.S. schools during the past thirty years is that teachers in the nation's classrooms have not reflected the racial and cultural backgrounds of the student populations they serve. In fact, as the student body increasingly diversifies, the teaching workforce seems to be moving in the opposite direction. Despite continued efforts to attract minority teachers, the AAEE reports that as of 2002, no real progress had been made. Additional surveys indicate that the number of minority teachers being certified and trained through college programs is not increasing to meet demand. The RNT also supports the claim that teachers of color are in demand in all subjects, grade areas, and geographic areas. To help address this demand, foundations are funding programs such as the Ford Foundation Consortia Project and DeWitt Wallace–Reader's Digest Fund's Pathways to Teaching Careers in order to attract and retain minority teachers.

DEMAND FOR SPECIAL EDUCATION TEACHERS

The increased understanding of various disabilities has resulted in the identification of larger numbers of students who can benefit from specialized instruction. Because these disabilities include both mental and physical conditions with varying degrees of severity, there is an increasing need for teacher specialization to address each group's particular needs. Students with special needs who receive appropriate instruction, support, and the necessary tools for their education have displayed considerable success in becoming contributing members of society.

The AAEE reports that nine out of ten special-education fields are experiencing considerable shortages. The RNT likewise reports that 73 percent of its survey respondents reported an immediate need for teachers trained in the various fields within special education. The National Clearinghouse for Careers in Education estimates that by 2010 the number of special education teachers will rise to more than 600,000, representing a 25 percent increase from 2000.

The trend toward including special education students in the regular education classroom has contributed to the rise in demand for special education teachers. Because of the demand for teachers who hold certification in both special education and regular education, master's programs across the nation are being designed to allow teachers to graduate with dual certification in a relatively short amount of time. In addition to dually certified teachers, other categories within special education that are experiencing high demand include emotional/behavioral disorders, severe disabilities, learning disabilities, mental retardation, visually impaired, and hearing impaired.

DEMAND FOR BILINGUAL TEACHERS

Numerous studies report a growing demand for teachers to assist the increasing numbers of students with limited English proficiency (referred to as LEP students). Not only must these educators teach in multiple languages, they must also increase their students' proficiency with English while simultaneously delivering the lesson content. Needless to say, teachers who have these language skills and are additionally certified are in great demand. The most common languages spoken by students with limited English are Spanish, Chinese (Cantonese and Mandarin), Korean, Arabic, Russian, Vietnamese, Navajo, and Tagalog, although teachers proficient in other languages are needed as well. According to the U.S. Department of Education, LEP enrollment has skyrocketed, increasing 95 percent from 1992 to 2002 (this contrasts with a 15 percent general enrollment increase).

DEMAND BY REGION

Although isolated shortages exist in specific areas in individual states and regions of the country, shortages are reflected in all geographic areas of the United States. Generally, urban and rural areas exhibit the highest levels of unmet demand. The AAEE offers some further insight into regional needs. For example, Washington State and Oregon are reportedly experiencing a disproportionate number of retirements. In California, efforts to reduce class size have resulted in a spike in the hiring of teachers at all levels. Other western states, such as Arizona, New Mexico, and Nevada, have such an extreme need for teachers, particularly math and science teachers, that they are hiring underqualified teachers through emergency procedures. Likewise, in rural areas in the Midwest, especially in the Dakotas, school systems are undertaking emergency measures, including the consolidation of schools, in order to compensate for a lack of funding and a loss of veteran teachers to retirement. Schools in the Southeast report shortages in all areas, but most severely in physics, biology, chemistry, and elementary school teaching. Cities in the Mid-Atlantic states from Maryland to New York are reporting considerable shortages in multiple areas, the most notable being special education. In New England, Rhode Island has an acute need for middle and high school teachers, while Connecticut is actively recruiting teachers in math, science, and computer proficiency.

Because of their large populations of students with limited English proficiency, states that have a particular need for teachers with skills in multiple languages are California, Arizona, Texas, Florida, Illinois, and New York. Although these states exhibit the highest percentages of students with special language needs, all states around the country are reporting growth in the number of LEP students.

TAPPING INTO THE HIGH DEMAND FOR TEACHERS

Evidence of the overwhelming demand for teachers can be found in the plentiful resources that connect teachers with schools. Online job banks offer teachers the opportunity to have their résumés reviewed by hundreds of schools nationwide, oftentimes free of charge. Individual states continually develop programs to attract teachers in areas of demand, often advertising these needs on their Web sites. In fact, the demand for all types of teachers is great in every type of school and in every geographic location.

If you are considering choices at the college level, such as choice of major or choice of specialization within education, the information included in this chapter can be used to your advantage. By choosing an area that is experiencing an acute shortage, you can open up a wider range of opportunities. However, regardless of the choices you make with regard to subject area or age level, your services as a teacher will be in demand. Good luck in landing that first teaching job!

A FINAL WORD

In short, education is a vast field with a variety of options available for a diverse group of people willing to take on challenges that can be immensely rewarding. However, to prepare yourself to enter this field, you will need to evaluate yourself in terms of your own personal, financial, and professional goals. In addition, the process of becoming a teacher requires a great deal of formal training.

As we have seen throughout this book, teaching represents a career that can be satisfying in a number of ways. The financial support, stability, and benefits associated with teaching combined with the time for pursuing secondary activities creates a situation that should be attractive to individuals of all backgrounds. The field of education is exciting partially because it is in a state of constant change. Schools are places where both teachers and students can come into direct contact with new ideas, progress in the sciences and the arts, and a wide range of cultures.

Distinct short- and long-term possibilities arise from a start in teaching. Your career path may lead in and out of teaching, or between areas within it. Regardless of your path, if you wish to continue growing and developing, education should remain a central theme for you during the course of your lifetime. Education in its many forms is truly an investment in yourself, in today's youth, and in the future of the planet.

By reading this book, you are beginning to understand yourself as a teacher! Teachers are constantly exploring the world and helping others do the same. An open mind and communication are key aspects of this lifelong process. Indeed, the skills, knowledge, and perspectives you will gain as you build a career as a teacher will remain beneficial to you no matter what turns your life takes.

Good luck!

GLOSSARY

accredited Meeting the requirements of a governing body, especially in regard to a college, university, or program within a college or university.

assessment The way a teacher measures a student's progress, effort, and understanding of the course material.

certification A formal acknowledgment from a state or city department of education that a teacher has completed a teacher training or master's program.

classroom management The way a teacher controls students in order to keep them focused on their study or other exercises.

content area A specific area of study. A content area is simply a subject such as English, math, science, art, and so on.

credential A general term that includes certification, license, and other diplomas that allow a teacher to be hired fully and legally.

curriculum The layout, or plan, for an entire course of study.

license In some states, the term "license" is identical to the definition of certification, but in others a license is more of a temporary permission to teach a specific subject area to a specific age group.

mentor A person who draws upon past experience to guide a younger person along a path that the mentor has already taken. A mentor takes an active role in advising and facilitating a person's development and progress toward a fairly specific goal.

multidisciplinary A curriculum attempting to use a variety of subject areas such as music, science, and history to teach aspects of a central theme.

paraprofessional An assistant teacher.

pedagogy The art and science of teaching.

postsecondary This term refers to programs for students who have completed secondary school.

provisional certificate A type of certificate granted to teachers who have completed all of the requirements of a master's degree teacher training course.

salary schedule A schedule showing salary increases that come with each year of experience.

secondary school More commonly known as high school. The term "primary" remains in more common usage for elementary schools.

tenure A status granted after a trial period to a teacher that gives him or her protection from dismissal.

FOR MORE INFORMATION

A LIST OF PROFESSIONALLY ACCREDITED COLLEGES AND UNIVERSITIES

Compiled by the National Council for Accreditation of Teacher Education

ALABAMA
Alabama A&M University
Alabama State University
Athens State University
Auburn University
Auburn University at
  Montgomery
Birmingham-Southern College
Jacksonville State University
Oakwood College (continued
  with conditions)
Samford University
Stillman College (accredited
  with provisions)
Troy State University
Troy State University
  Dothan (accredited
  with conditions)
Tuskegee University
University of Alabama (contin-
  ued with conditions)
University of Alabama at
  Birmingham
University of Montevallo
University of North
  Alabama
University of South
  Alabama
University of West Alabama

ARKANSAS
Arkansas State University

Arkansas Tech University
Harding University
Henderson State
  University
Hendrix College
John Brown University
Lyon College
Ouachita Baptist University
Philander Smith College
Southern Arkansas
  University
University of Arkansas at
  Fayetteville
University of Arkansas at
  Little Rock
University of Arkansas at
  Monticello
University of Arkansas at
  Pine Bluff
University of Central
  Arkansas
University of the Ozarks
Williams Baptist College

CALIFORNIA
Azusa Pacific University
California Lutheran
  University
California State University–
  Bakersfield
California State University–
  Dominguez Hills

California State
University-Fresno
California State
University-Fullerton
California State
University-Hayward
California State University at
Long Beach
California State University-
Los Angeles
California State
University-Northridge
California State University-
San Bernardino
California State University-
San Marcos
California State
University-Stanislaus
Loyola Marymount
University
San Diego State University
San Francisco State
University
San Jose State University
(continued with conditions)
Stanford University
University of the Pacific

COLORADO
Adams State College
Colorado State University
Metropolitan State College
of Denver
University of Colorado
at Boulder
University of Colorado at
Colorado Springs
University of Colorado
at Denver

CONNECTICUT
Central Connecticut
State University
Eastern Connecticut State
University (provisionally

accredited at the
advanced level)
University of Connecticut
University of Hartford

DELAWARE
Delaware State University
University of Delaware
Wesley College

DISTRICT OF COLUMBIA
American University
Catholic University
of America
Gallaudet University
George Washington
University
Howard University

FLORIDA
Bethune-Cookman College
Florida A&M University
Florida Atlantic University
Florida International
University
Florida Memorial College
Florida State University
Stetson University
University of Central
Florida
University of Florida
University of Miami
University of North Florida
University of South Florida
University of West Florida

GEORGIA
Albany State University
Armstrong Atlantic State
University
Atlanta Christian College
Augusta State University
Berry College
Brenau University
Clark Atlanta University

Clayton College and State
University
Columbus State University
Emory University
Fort Valley State University
(accredited with probation)
Georgia College and State
University
Georgia Southern University
Georgia Southwestern State
University
Georgia State University
Kennesaw State University
North Georgia College &
State University
Spelman College (accredited
with conditions)
State University of
West Georgia
University of Georgia
Valdosta State University

HAWAII
University of Hawaii
at Manoa

IDAHO
Boise State University
Idaho State University
Lewis–Clark State College
Northwest Nazarene College
University of Idaho

ILLINOIS
Augustana College
Bradley University
Chicago State University
Concordia University
DePaul University
Eastern Illinois University
Elmhurst College
Governors State University
Illinois State University
Lewis University
Loyola University Chicago

National Louis University
Northeastern Illinois
University
Northern Illinois University
Olivet Nazarene University
Roosevelt University
Saint Xavier
Southern Illinois University at
Carbondale (advanced level
continued with conditions)
Southern Illinois University at
Edwardsville
Western Illinois University
Wheaton College

INDIANA
Anderson University
Ball State University
(advanced level continued
with conditions)
Bethel College
Butler University
DePauw University
Franklin College
Goshen College
Grace College
Hanover College
Huntington College
Indiana State University
Indiana University at
Bloomington/Indianapolis
Indiana University East
Indiana University Kokomo
(initial accreditation continued
with conditions, advanced level
continued with probation)
Indiana University
Northwest
Indiana University–Purdue
University Fort Wayne
(advanced level continued
with conditions)
Indiana University
South Bend
Indiana University Southeast

Indiana Wesleyan University
Manchester College
Marian College
Oakland City University
Purdue University
Purdue University Calumet
Saint Joseph's College
Saint Mary-of-the-Woods College
Saint Mary's College
Taylor University
University of Evansville
University of Indianapolis
University of Saint Francis
University of Southern
  Indiana
Valparaiso University
Wabash College

IOWA
Graceland University
Luther College
Morningside College
Northwestern College
Wartburg College

KANSAS
Baker University
Benedictine College
Bethany College
Emporia State University
Fort Hays State University
  (continued with probation)
Friends University (continued
  with probation)
Kansas State University
Kansas Wesleyan University
McPherson College
Ottawa University
Pittsburg State University
Southwestern College
University of Kansas
University of Saint Mary
Washburn University
  of Topeka

Wichita State University
  continued with probation)

KENTUCKY
Asbury College
Bellarmine College
Berea College
Eastern Kentucky University
Kentucky State University
Morehead State University
Murray State University
Northern Kentucky
  University
Spalding University
Transylvania University
University of Kentucky
University of Louisville
Western Kentucky University

LOUISIANA
Dillard University
Grambling State University
Louisiana State University and
  A&M College
Louisiana State University
  in Shreveport
Louisiana Tech University
McNeese State University
Nicholls State University
Northwestern State University
  of Louisiana
Southeastern Louisiana
  University
Southern University at
  Baton Rouge (continued
  with probation)
Southern University
  New Orleans
University of Louisiana
  at Lafayette
University of Louisiana
  at Monroe
University of New Orleans
Xavier University

MAINE

University of Maine
University of Maine at
  Farmington
University of Southern
  Maine

MARYLAND

Bowie State University
College of Notre Dame
  of Maryland
Coppin State College
Frostburg State University
Johns Hopkins University
Loyola College
Morgan State University
Salisbury State University
Towson University
University of Maryland,
  Baltimore County
University of Maryland,
  College Park
University of Maryland Eastern
  Shore (provisionally accredited
  at initial level)

MASSACHUSETTS

Boston College
Bridgewater State College
Fitchburg State College
Salem State College
University of Massachusetts—
  Amherst
University of Massachusetts—
  Boston
University of Massachusetts—
  Lowell
Westfield State College
  (accredited with provisions
  at advanced level)
Wheelock College

MICHIGAN

Andrews University
Calvin College

Central Michigan University
Concordia College
Eastern Michigan University
Grand Valley State University
Hope College
Madonna University
Marygrove College (accredited
  with conditions)
Northern Michigan University
Oakland University
Saginaw Valley State
  University
Spring Arbor College
Western Michigan University

MINNESOTA

Augsburg College
College of St. Benedict and St.
  John's University
Concordia University
Gustavus Adolphus College
Hamline University
Minnesota State
  University, Mankato
Minnesota State
  University, Moorhead
Saint Cloud State University
Saint Olaf College
University of Minnesota
  at Duluth
University of Minnesota at Morris
University of Minnesota at
  Twin Cities
University of Saint
  Thomas
Winona State University
  (accredited with conditions
  at advanced level)

MISSISSIPPI

Alcorn State University
Delta State University
Jackson State University
Millsaps College
Mississippi College

Mississippi State University
Mississippi University
  for Women
Mississippi Valley State
  University
University of Mississippi
University of Southern
  Mississippi

MISSOURI
Central Missouri State
  University
Drury College
Evangel University
Harris–Stowe State College
Lincoln University
Maryville University
Missouri Southern
  State College
Missouri Western State College
Northwest Missouri State
  University
Saint Louis University
Southeast Missouri State
  University
Southwest Missouri State
  University
Truman State University
University of
  Missouri–Columbia
University of Missouri at
  Kansas City (accredited with
  conditions at initial level,
  accredited with probation at
  advanced level)
University of Missouri–
  Saint Louis

MONTANA
Montana State
  University–Bozeman
Montana State
  University–Billings
Montana State
  University–Northern

University of Montana
University of Montana–Western

NEBRASKA
Chadron State College
Concordia University
Creighton University
Dana College
Doane College
Hastings College
Nebraska Wesleyan University
Peru State College (continued
  with probation)
Union College
University of Nebraska
  at Kearney
University of Nebraska
  at Lincoln
University of Nebraska at Omaha
Wayne State College

NEVADA
University of Nevada at
  Las Vegas
University of Nevada at Reno

NEW HAMPSHIRE
Keene State College
Plymouth State College

NEW JERSEY
College of New Jersey
Kean University
Montclair State University
New Jersey City University
Rider University
Rowan University
William Paterson University
  of New Jersey

NEW MEXICO
Eastern New Mexico State
  University
New Mexico Highlands
  University

New Mexico State University
University of New Mexico
Western New Mexico
   University

NEW YORK
Bank Street College of
   Education
Buffalo State College
Five Towns College
Fordham University
Hofstra University
Iona College I & A
Lehman College CUNY
Niagara University
The Sage Colleges I & A
State University College
   at Fredonia
St. Bonaventure University
St.Thomas Aquinas University
SUNY Brockport (accredited
   with provisions)
SUNY New Paltz
SUNY Oneonta
SUNY Oswego
SUNY Potsdam I & A

NORTH CAROLINA
Appalachian State University
Barton College
Belmont Abbey College
Bennett College
Campbell University
Catawba College
Chowan College
Davidson College
Duke University
East Carolina University
Elizabeth City State University
   (continued accreditation with
   conditions at initial level,
   accredited with provisions at
   advanced level)
Elon University

Fayetteville State University
Gardner–Webb University
Greensboro College
Guilford College
High Point University
Johnson C. Smith University
Lees–McRae College
Lenoir–Rhyne College
Livingstone College
Mars Hill College
Meredith College
Methodist College (continued
   with probation)
Montreat College
North Carolina A&T State
   University
North Carolina Central
   University
North Carolina State
   University
North Carolina Wesleyan College
Pfeiffer University
Queens College of Charlotte
   (continued with conditions)
Saint Andrews
   Presbyterian College
Saint Augustine's College
Salem College
Shaw University
University of North Carolina
   at Asheville
University of North Carolina
   at Chapel Hill (accreditation
   with conditions)
University of North Carolina
   at Charlotte
University of North Carolina
   at Greensboro
University of North Carolina
   at Pembroke
University of North Carolina
   at Wilmington
Wake Forest University
Warren Wilson College

Western Carolina University
Wingate University (accredited
  with conditions)
Winston-Salem State University

NORTH DAKOTA
Dickinson State University
Mayville State University
Minot State University
North Dakota State
  University
University of North Dakota
Valley City State University

OHIO
Ashland University
Baldwin-Wallace College
Bowling Green State
  University
Capital University
Cleveland State University
John Carroll University
Kent State University
Miami University
Ohio Northern University
Ohio State University
Ohio University
Otterbein College
Shawnee State University
University of Akron
University of Cincinnati
University of Dayton
University of Findlay
University of Toledo
Wittenburg University
Wright State University
Youngstown State University

OKLAHOMA
Cameron University
East Central University
Langston University
  (continued with conditions)
Northeastern State University

Northwestern Oklahoma State
  University
Oklahoma Baptist University
Oklahoma Christian University
  of Science and Arts
Oklahoma Panhandle
  State University
Oklahoma State University
Oklahoma Wesleyan University
Oral Roberts University
Southeastern Oklahoma
  State University
Southern Nazarene University
  (continued with conditions)
Southwestern Oklahoma
  State University
University of Central
  Oklahoma
University of Oklahoma
University of Science and Arts
  of Oklahoma
University of Tulsa

OREGON
Oregon State University
Portland State University
University of Portland
Western Oregon University

PENNSYLVANIA
Bloomsburg University
  of Pennsylvania
California University
  of Pennsylvania
Cheyney University
  (continued with conditions)
Clarion University of
  Pennsylvania
East Stroudsburg University
Edinboro University
Indiana University
  of Pennsylvania
Marywood University
Pennsylvania State University

Temple University
University of Scranton
West Chester University

RHODE ISLAND
Rhode Island College
(conditions at advanced level)

SOUTH CAROLINA
Anderson College
Benedict College
Claflin University
Clemson University
Coastal Carolina University
College of Charleston
Columbia College
Francis Marion University
Furman University
Lander University
Newberry College
Presbyterian College
South Carolina State University
University of South
Carolina
Winthrop University

SOUTH DAKOTA
Augustana College
Black Hills State University
Dakota State University
Northern State University
South Dakota State
University
University of Sioux Falls
University of South Dakota

TENNESSEE
Austin Peay State University
Belmont University
Carson–Newman College
Freed–Hardeman University
LeMoyne–Owen College
Lipscomb University
Middle Tennessee
State University

Milligan College
Southern Adventist University
Tennessee State University
Tennessee Technological
University
Union University
University of Memphis
University of Tennessee
at Chattanooga
University of Tennessee
at Knoxville
University of Tennessee
at Martin
Vanderbilt University

TEXAS
Baylor University (accredited
with conditions at initial
level and accredited with
probation at advanced level)
Prairie View A & M University
Sam Houston
State University
Stephen F. Austin State
University
Texas A & M University
Texas Tech University
Trinity University
University of Houston
University of Houston
at Clear Lake
University of North Texas
University of Texas at
Arlington (provisionally
accredited)

UTAH
Brigham Young University
(continued with probation)
Southern Utah University
Utah State University
Weber State University

VERMONT
University of Vermont

VIRGINIA
The College of William and
Mary (accredited with
conditions)
Eastern Mennonite
University
George Mason University
Hampton University
James Madison University
Liberty University
(accredited with provisions)
Longwood College
Marymount University
Norfolk State University
Old Dominion University
Radford University
University of Virginia
Virginia Commonwealth
University
Virginia Polytechnic Institute
and State University
Virginia State University
Virginia Union University

WASHINGTON
Central Washington University
Eastern Washington
University
Gonzaga University
Pacific Lutheran University
Seattle Pacific University
Seattle University
University of Puget Sound
University of Washington,
Seattle
Washington State University
Western Washington
University
Whitworth College

WEST VIRGINIA
Alderson–Broaddus College

Bethany College
Bluefield State College
Concord College
Fairmont State College
Glenville State College
Marshall University
Shepherd College
University of Charleston
West Liberty State College
West Virginia State College
West Virginia University
West Virginia University
at Parkersburg
West Virginia Wesleyan
College

WISCONSIN
Alverno College
Cardinal Stritch University
Edgewood College
(continued with probation)
Marian College of Fond du Lac
Marquette University
University of Wisconsin at La
Crosse (continued with
probation)
University of Wisconsin
at Oshkosh
University of Wisconsin
at Platteville
University of Wisconsin at
River Falls
University of Wisconsin at
Whitewater (continued
with probation)
Viterbo University

WYOMING
University of Wyoming

PUERTO RICO
University of Puerto Rico

EDUCATION ASSOCIATIONS

American Federation of Teachers
555 New Jersey Avenue NW
Washington, DC 20001
(202) 879-4400
Web site: http://www.aft.org

American Library Association
50 East Huron
Chicago, IL 60611
(800) 545-2433
Web site: http://www.ala.org

Council for Exceptional Children
1110 North Glebe Road, Suite 300
Arlington, VA 22201-5704
(888) CEC-SPED (232-7733)
Web site: http://www.cec.sped.org

International Society for Technology in Education
1710 Rhode Island Avenue NW, Suite 900
Washington, DC 20036
(202) 861-7777
Web site: http://www.iste.org

National Association of Biology Teachers (NABT)
12030 Sunrise Valley Drive, Suite 110
Reston, VA 20191
(800) 406-0775
Web site: http://www.nabt.org

National Association of Professional Educators
900 17th Street, Suite 300
Washington, DC 20006
E-mail: acrocke@tenet.edu or freebird@mindspring.com

National Council for the Social Studies
8555 Sixteenth Street, Suite 500
Silver Spring, MD 20910
(301) 588-1800
Web site: http://www.ncss.org

National Council for Teachers of Mathematics
1906 Association Drive
Reston, VA 20191-1502
(703) 620-9840
Web site: http://www.nctm.org

National Education Association
1201 16th Street NW
Washington, DC 20036-3290
(202) 833-4000
Web site: http://www.nea.org

National Middle School Association
4151 Executive Parkway, Suite 300
Westerville, OH 43081
(800) 528-NMSA (6672)
E-mail: info@NMSA.org

National Science Teachers Association
1840 Wilson Boulevard
Arlington, VA 22201-3000
(703) 243-7100
Web site: http://www.nsta.org

FOR FURTHER READING

Burke, Lisa Maria. *Teacher's Ultimate Planning Guide.* Thousand Oaks, CA: Corwin Press, 2002.

Echaore-McDavid, Susan. *Career Opportunities in Education.* New York: Checkmark Books, 2001.

Edelfelt, Roy. *Careers in Education.* Chicago: NTC/Contemporary Publishing Company, 1998.

Feirsen, Robert, and Seth Weitzman. *How to Get the Teaching Job You Want.* Sterling, VA: Stylus Publishing, 2004.

Steffy, Betty E., ed. *Life Cycle of the Career Teacher.* Thousand Oaks, CA: Corwin Press, 1999.

BIBLIOGRAPHY

Brolin, Donn E. *Career Education: A Functional Life Skills Approach*. Upper Saddle River, NJ: Prentice Hall, 1995.

Burke, Lisa Maria. *The Teacher's Ultimate Planning Guide*. Thousand Oaks, CA: Corwin Press, 2002.

Echaore-McDavid, Susan. *Career Opportunities in Education*. New York: Checkmark Books, 2001.

Edelfelt, Roy. *Careers in Education*. Chicago: NTC/Contemporary Publishing Company, 1998.

Editors of VGM Career Horizons. *Résumés for Education Careers*. Chicago: VGM Career Horizons, 1999.

Feirsen, Robert, and Seth Weitzman. *How to Get the Teaching Job You Want*. Sterling, VA: Stylus Publishing, 2004.

Gray, Kenneth C., and Edwin L. Herr. *Workforce Education: The Basics*. London: Pearson Allyn & Bacon, 1997.

Heward, William L. *Exceptional Children: An Introduction to Special Education*. Upper Saddle River, NJ: Merrill/Prentice Hall, 2003.

Kronenfeld, Jennie, and Marcia Whicker. *Getting an Academic Job*. London: Sage Publications, 1997.

Lyons, Nona, ed. *With Portfolio in Hand*. New York: Teachers College Press, 1998.

INDEX

ACKNOWLEDGMENTS

Special thanks to Hunter College in New York City, New York.

ABOUT THE AUTHOR

J. Barrett Heaton has been a student and a teacher at a variety of schools, both public and private. He holds an M.F.A. from the San Francisco Art Institute and is currently completing his master's of education degree at Hunter College. He lives with his wife and daughter in Brooklyn, New York.